AS TIME GOES BY
A Life's Journey from Casablanca *July 2014*

To my sweet niece Lucienne
With all my heart !
Uncle Sidney

Printed May 2014

Cover by: MWdesign, mwdezine2@sbcglobal.net

To my sweetheart Juliette, the love of my life for 66 years, my wonderful wife of 55 years and the centerpiece of my family.

For every man the death of a wife is traumatic. For our family, Juliette was the beacon of light that shined on us all. She had a beautiful smile for every joy, a tear for every sorrow and an encouragement for every dream.

She was and will always be,
"La femme de ma vie" (the woman of my life).

ACKNOWLEDGEMENTS

I am deeply grateful to my three beloved daughters, Colette Grey, Josiane Feigon and Sandi Bouhadana. During the period of *Shiva* after Juliette's passing, my daughters encouraged me to write my life story to perpetuate Juliette's memory as the beautiful and special wife, sister, mother and grandmother that she was.

My heartfelt gratitude also goes to my sister-in law Yvonne Gabay, Juliette's sister and best friend. Yvonne has always been like a sister to me and her love and support after Juliette's passing has been a source of great comfort to me and my children. Yvonne, along with many of my dear nieces and nephews, urged me to start writing as they felt confident that such an undertaking could help me deal with my grief at this very difficult time in my life.

The story of the Chriqui family would not have been possible without the efforts, patience and love from our beloved parents Judah and Simha Chriqui. We were indeed very lucky to have been raised by them. Their faith in humanity was expressed in everything they did. They taught us the meaning of unconditional love and the importance of helping each other. Their marriage lasted for 66 years until my father died in 1977. We grew up witnessing their daily struggles and sacrifices to give us a good education and to steer us in the right direction, particularly during times of hardship. My father was full of wisdom and integrity, and my mother was gentle, courageous, kind and generous. Their devotion to their children and their respect for others are gifts we all inherited and passed on to our own children and grandchildren.

SPECIAL THANKS

The person I owe the most for the completion of this project is my dear and beautiful niece Nicole Chriqui Rivera. Though I had written some material in the months after Juliette's passing, several years had passed since I stopped writing and I was about to abandon the project altogether. I was searching for something or someone to shake me up a little -- that person was Nicole.

Nicole read my notes and volunteered to help me complete the project. She transformed the already written material into a coherent narrative and in so doing, gave me the incentive I needed to continue. Her inquisitive mind, organizational skills, enthusiasm and keen interest in my story allowed me to focus more clearly on my past. Together we developed a comprehensive and hopefully interesting account of events.

Through over a year of meetings, phone calls and emails, I provided Nicole with written notes and an oral history of my life which she revised and edited into the pages you are reading today. She also prepared the manuscript for printing, including the selection and layout of the pictures.

I am very grateful for all the time and effort Nicole has devoted to this project. Her involvement was instrumental in the completion of this book.

PROLOGUE

After the loss of my wife my entire life came to a standstill. I felt empty and lost. The impact of no longer having her at my side was enormous. I experienced various stages of confusion and crisis. I had never thought that we could be separated one day and was totally unprepared when it happened.

A few days after her passing while looking through some old papers, I came across a box of letters that she had kept hidden for decades. I had written these letters to her over the course of many years before we were married. I was astonished to discover that she had saved them for over fifty years! This special gift unleashed a flood of memories as I read about my life as a young man. These letters, along with encouragement and prodding from friends and family, inspired me to write my life story.

Spanning a period of more than seven decades and extending to four continents, I will detail some of the major events and people who have shaped my life and accompanied me during my memorable journey. Also included are some major historical events which took place during those years, including those that I personally experienced in Morocco and later in other countries.

As a Sephardic Jew, I am a descendent of the large number of Jews who were expelled from Spain in 1492 and who settled in North Africa. In his book, "The Grandees," Stephen Birmingham writes that in medieval Spain and Portugal, the Sephardic Jews were the nobility of Jewry. They were not only the bankers and financial advisers to the royal courts, but also Spain's scientists, physicians, jurists, philosophers and poets. When the Sultan of Turkey heard that Ferdinand and Isabella had ordered the Jews expelled from Spain, he commented, "The King of Spain must have lost his mind. He is expelling his best subjects." Yet the Jews were expelled and Spain has never been the same.

Prior to 1912 when Morocco became a French protectorate, it was very much a third world country with little in the way of infrastructure or educational opportunities. The French brought the modern world to Morocco: roads, running water, hospitals, schools, etc. They also brought elegant Art Deco architecture, making Casablanca one of the most beautiful and vibrant cities in the world (see page 200 for more on the architectural history of Casablanca).

If not for the French, I and my siblings would have had little opportunity for education. The regular French schools were mainly for the French and Europeans, including European Jews; only a small number of Moroccans were allowed. However, the *Alliance Israelite Universelle*, a French Jewish organization, built and operated several schools specifically for Moroccan Jews. Though we spoke Arabic as our first language, we were schooled in French and Hebrew. Most of the professors were Jews of Spanish origin who came to Morocco from Turkey.

At the time I lived there, Morocco was home to a vibrant community of approximately 350,000 Jews. After the independence of Morocco in 1956, most left the country and went mainly to Israel, France, Canada and the United States. Today, there are just 2,500 Jews remaining in Morocco. I consider myself to be a link from the era when exiled Jews from Spain lived in Morocco for centuries, to their departure from Morocco in the 1950's.

In writing this memoir, I have an opportunity to share their values, beliefs and traditions with my children, grandchildren and future family descendents. It is important for the youth to know more about their families' past and the struggles that their parents and grandparents endured. It is rewarding to know that I will be leaving a legacy for my descendents, with a humble hope that my story will serve as an inspiration in their own lives.

PART ONE

MOROCCO 1925 - 1948

Chapter 1

I was born on December 9, 1925 in Casablanca, Morocco, the seventh of nine children of the Chriqui family. The Chriqui name has existed in Morocco since the 15th century and is of oriental origin. It means "the wind from the East," (in Spanish *Delevante* and in Hebrew *Mizrahi*). The greatest of gifts that a man receives at birth is free and has no conditions - his name. It is up to him to honor or tarnish it.

My father, Judah D. Chriqui, was the youngest son of David Chriqui, a rich, local trader from Rabat who had five sons and two daughters. Born in 1892, Judah was a quiet, reserved man who did not show emotion. Though he was proud of his family and would brag to his friends about his children, he never spoke a word of praise or encouragement to us. In 1911 when he was 19, he married 16 year old Simha, my mother.

Simha was the eldest daughter of Rabbi Abraham Hadida and Freha Laredo. Simha was exuberant with love and affection, and ruled the roost at home. Because Grandfather Abraham had no sons, he gave my mother a good Hebrew education. My mother was only 4 when Grandpa Abraham would carry her on his shoulders to an all-boys synagogue in Rabat. Simha was a quick learner and had already absorbed several of her father's Hebrew books at a very young age. From her father, Simha inherited a great deal of compassion and wisdom.

My maternal grandmother Freha Laredo, "Ema Freha" as we called her, was small in stature but quite energetic and full of life. She dressed in the traditional clothing of the time, essentially embroidered blouses and long skirts. She was stern, disciplined and very modest. I remember she would hide her tiny body under several large skirts. Both maternal grandparents came from religious, orthodox families who had raised their children with strong Jewish principles and a great respect for Jewish traditions.

Grandfather Abraham was an adventurer. In the early nineteenth century he joined a group of young Jewish men who went to South America because it was so difficult to find good jobs in Morocco. Northern Brazil was rich in rubber, cocoa and sugar and the trade of these commodities provided the Moroccan immigrants with good salaries, enabling them to send money home to their families. When he first left, he had a wife and one daughter, my mother. He would return periodically but because it took months to travel from Brazil to Morocco, he would be gone for years at a time and was once away for a period of seven years. By the time he returned to Morocco for good, he'd had two additional daughters, Messoda and Sasbona. Once back in Rabat, he pursued religious studies and became a well respected rabbi.

My paternal grandparents died when I was very young so I have no memories of them. My father had six siblings, four of which died when I was young. Therefore my only recollection of my father's family is of two uncles, Shalom and Abraham Chriqui. These uncles were very reserved and did not maintain much of a relationship with our family. By contrast, relatives from our Mom's family, the Amelard and Asseraf families, were very exuberant and loving and we saw them often.

A bizarre coincidence is that my Uncle Abraham Chriqui had eight sons and one daughter, and my mother's youngest sister Sasbona Asseraf had eight daughters and one son! (Sasbona died in Israel a few years ago at the age of 102).

In 1979 when I was in Israel, I visited my Uncle Shalom who shared with me few stories about the Chriqui's in Rabat. Apparently we were known as the "Dar Sabone" family, meaning the "House of Soap" family because the Chriqui's had a very successful soap business in Morocco. The three Chriqui brothers had inherited large sums of money from this business and only my father had lost his share by trusting a cousin on a business deal that went bad. To this day, some of my father's nephews still have large real estate holdings in Casablanca.

Chapter 2

My parents spent their youth and the first part of their marriage in the *Mellah*, the walled Jewish quarter in Rabat. The *Mellah* was a melting pot of the well-off and the poor. Wealthier families had larger, more elaborate houses, and families would pass houses down from one generation to the other. Some of the streets ("*derb*" in Arabic) were so narrow that you could touch the houses on either side without fully outstretching your arms.

Once a year usually around Passover, the houses would be whitewashed, both inside and out; the streets would get whitewashed as well. Sometimes a colored pigment would be added so that not everything was white. This "spring cleaning" also involved cutting open the woolen mattresses to check for bugs, putting them out in the sun to be sanitized, then closing them up for another year.

Houses usually shared a courtyard, with individual living quarters off the courtyard. At the time my eldest sister Sultana

Renée was born in 1913, the Dery and Chriqui families lived across a courtyard from one another. Her future husband Albert was also born there, six years prior in 1907. When Albert's mother saw Renée, she was so enthralled with the baby's beauty that she proclaimed Renée would marry her son. This "prediction" actually happened 20 years later!

My parents' education was limited to Jewish studies in Hebrew. Though they could read and write Hebrew, they did not speak it. Hebrew as a spoken language was not widespread at that time, and was not revived until the formation of Israel. The spoken language was Arabic, but they could neither read nor write in Arabic. So they would write using Hebrew letters to "sound out" Arabic words. My father taught himself French in his late teens and could eventually read and write in French, albeit with grammatical and spelling errors.

In the early years of their marriage, my father had a very high level job with a large importer of tea and sugar, frequently travelling to France for the procurement of goods. On one of those trips, he brought the first two-wheeled bicycle from France to Rabat.

Five of their nine children were born in Rabat: Sultana Renée, David, Esther, Clothilde (Claudia) and Jacques. The first two children enjoyed the benefits of prosperity such as music lessons and nice clothes. Surrounded by many children and a large extended family, my parents led a happy life in Rabat.

In 1922 when Jacques was 1 year old, the family relocated sixty miles south to Casablanca, which was a larger city. My father always stressed location and education, so I believe the move was for better opportunities in Casablanca. The remaining four children were born in Casablanca: Marie, Salomon (Sidney), André and Maurice.

We were a very close family, always helping each other while growing up. My mother was the pillar of the family and played a major role in our upbringing. She was strong willed, determined and full of affection. A religious woman, she prayed every morning, concluding by opening the window and looking up to the sky to pray to *Hashem* (God) that she never see any harm befall her children. As I grew up, my family's Jewish roots and traditions played an important role in shaping my values. My older brothers and sisters were strong role models and I loved every one of them dearly.

Sometime in the early 1920's, my father lost his job. He subsequently opened a business with a cousin, who unilaterally took over the business and terminated the partnership while my father was away in Europe. Because their association had taken place on a verbal agreement, my father had no legal recourse.

Having lost all the money inherited from my grandfather, my father was in a desperate situation and had to sell some of my mother's jewelry to support the family. He never recovered from the shock of the betrayal and subsequent financial devastation. He tried a wholesale fruit and vegetable business for awhile, but when that didn't succeed, he stopped working altogether. From that time forward, he spent his days at the horse track or playing cards with friends in the local cafe. We had been raised to have respect for our parents, regardless of the circumstances, so none of us ever reproached our father for not working. My mother was fiercely determined to hold the family together no matter what, which is her legacy to this day.

André was always chosen to do the errands. When he was around 9, he was running up the stairs with two glass jugs of wine he had just purchased for Friday night dinner, when he slipped. The glass broke and severely cut his right arm. I came home to find him sitting on the stairs dazed and bleeding profusely. I scooped him up and carried him to a clinic, dripping blood the whole way. This clinic would not touch you if you had no money to pay for their services. I banged on the door and shouted that my father was a rich man and they would be in big trouble if they didn't treat my brother. In reality, my father had no money and the bill was never paid.

When they completed high school, my siblings David and Esther became the main breadwinners, and as each of us got jobs, we too participated in supporting the family. Esther had a steady job as a secretary and switchboard operator for a large European company. Esther was kind, generous, affectionate and very family oriented. She also had a mind of her own and was often at odds with everyone else. Until she married and had children, all her earnings went to support the family.

David became the de facto head of the household. At one time, David worked in a deli and would bring home what he could, to supplement the family meals. He bought himself a motorcycle to get around town. One day when he was bringing home a jar of mustard from the deli, he had a mishap on the bike and the jar broke, covering the bike in mustard.

David was patient, quiet, handsome, and full of wisdom and charm. He was always ready to assist us in any way possible, be it financial or otherwise. No matter what we did as kids, he never punished us, which is illustrated in the following story.

I would often play ball in the street with other boys from the neighborhood. When I was about 7, there was a middle-aged delivery man who didn't like us at all. He would call us names, chase us, take our ball, etc. One day he came to deliver soft drinks to a neighborhood market and left his horse and cart unattended. Not thinking what would happen, we took a rod, put a hot pepper on the end, lifted the horse's tail and stuck the rod into the horse. The horse went berserk, bucking and thrashing about, which completely destroyed the cart and wreaked havoc in the street.

We all scattered and I ran home as if nothing had happened. When David came home and asked if I had been involved in the disturbance, I eventually admitted my guilt. David did not raise his voice and did not reprimand me. He simply declared that everyone who had been affected would need to be reimbursed for their losses.

David, 1940's   *Esther, 1940's*

Chapter 3

One of my earliest memories is the wedding of my eldest sister Renée in March 1933 when I was 8 years old. Renée married Albert Dery, who had lived across the courtyard from my family when they were both children. Albert was now a dashing young man who was making a very good living in real estate. Every week, he would drive an hour from Rabat to Casablanca to see Renée. In Casablanca, he would hire a horse drawn carriage for their dates. Since it was not proper for a young girl to go out alone, Esther would accompany them. Claudia would get dressed up and run after the carriage because she wanted to go too!

Albert and Renée were madly in love and wed when Renée was about 20. My mother was 38 at the time, pregnant with her 9th child, Maurice. She and my father had their hands full with eight children and one on the way, yet some of the festivities were held in our home, a large apartment on Rue Dohue behind the Casablanca Central Market.

I clearly remember that day, particularly finding a large wallet full of French currency in the hallway of our building. I gave the wallet to my Dad and to this day, I don't know what he did with it. I would like to think that he tried to return the wallet to its rightful owner, but with the impending wedding and our very tight finances, it's more probable that he considered it "manna from heaven".

Albert and Renée's wedding was my first experience with the traditional *Henna*. Sephardic Jews, particularly North Africans, begin wedding festivities several days before the actual ceremony with an elaborate party called *Henna* where the bride wears an elaborately embroidered velvet dress adorned with pearls and other jewels. Often this dress is a family heirloom, passed down through the generations. After guests share a meal, henna dye is applied to each woman's palm, symbolizing fertility and protection against the evil eye.

After Renée's *Henna*, all the guests were driven from Casablanca to Rabat in two large buses. Songs and humorous stories were provided along the way by Moise Azoulay, known as "Moise le

Coiffeur" (Moise the Hairdresser), a close family friend. (Moise's son is the well known Moroccan painter, Guillaume Azoulay.) In Rabat, Albert Dery had a dinner-dance party for a large gathering of family and friends of the Derys.

Renée (left) in her Henna dress, with two cousins, 1933

Albert Dery and Renée on their wedding day, 1933

That same year, brother Jacques, who was 12 at the time, would walk with me to school, La Fonciere (a French school), where we were both students. I was, and still am, very close to Jacques. Jacques was a very bright student who skipped a grade or two, but he was also a bit of a rebel who wanted to do what he wanted, when he wanted.

On many occasions, Jacques would take me to the local beach instead of to school. He was an avid swimmer and loved the ocean. He would ask me to keep silent about our escapades and to sit on the sand and watch his belongings. I used this time to read French books, a habit which I have kept to this day.

Because of our frequent absences, the school principal informed my father that he was expelling us. The family had to move to a different part of Casablanca so that we could continue our studies at another school, the *Alliance Israelite Narcisse Leven* school, where we rapidly progressed.

We moved to a large apartment in a modern building at 81 Place de Verdun. Our apartment was on the fifth floor and though the building had an elevator, it never worked. The building housed about twenty Jewish families, and everyone knew everyone.

81 Place de Verdun in Casablanca

Place de Verdun was a gathering place for teenagers and young adults. One corner of the building was located on Rue Lacepede, which was lined with modern apartment buildings inhabited by middle-income Jewish families. Also on Rue Lacepede was the *Cercle de L'Alliance*, a Jewish club where young men and women gathered to discuss a variety of subjects relating to politics, sports, movies, dances, etc. It was a great place to live and I made lifelong friends there.

At the time the last of my siblings, Maurice, was born in June 1933, many of us were still kids. Respectively our ages were as follows: André was 4; I was 8; Marie, 10; Jacques, 12; Claudia 14; Esther 17; David, 19 and Renée, who had just married and moved to Rabat, was 20.

Renée at age 28, 1941

Chapter 4

Life was not easy in the 30's and 40's, particularly during WWII (1939 to 1944). There was a time when I didn't own a single pair of long pants and would be teased at school because of my short pants. New clothing was not readily available but even if it had been, we couldn't afford it. My mother would ask family friends for their old clothes, which she would have a tailor alter by turning them inside out. Shoes would be passed down from oldest to youngest, so by the time Maurice got the shoes, the soles were completely worn out and had separated from the leather, so they "clapped" when he walked.

As kids, we would play with whatever we could find on the street. One popular game, called Kiney, was to take a piece of wood about 8" long and taper it at both ends. This tapered stick would be placed on a small rock, then hit with another piece of wood, which would cause the stick to fly up in the air. The goal was to catch the stick in the air. Thinking back, it's amazing that no one lost an eye!

Meat and fish were expensive, so we ate mostly fruits and vegetables (salads, soups) which were affordable and plentiful. Since we had no refrigerator, my mother would walk to the outdoor market every day, offering a few francs to local beggars to help her carry the bags home and up the five flights of stairs to our apartment.

On the few occasions when we would get say, a chicken, my mother would always serve David first since he was the head of the household. Then she would divide the remaining meat among the rest of us. André would always end up with the wings, so much so that he asked if she wanted him to fly! My mother would serve herself last, by which time there was no meat left. She basically subsisted on lettuce and bread.

Maurice loved eggs ("*baida*" in Arabic) and little else. When he was about 8 or so, he would go into the kitchen, peek under the pot lids, and declare that he didn't like what was inside, regardless of what it was. "I want baida" he would demand, with no regard for whether there were any eggs in the house. During the war, getting eggs required standing in long ration lines, but Maurice would insist on eggs nonetheless.

My mother would cure many pounds of large olives, place them in a jar and put them in the hall closet. We would come home from school every day, fish out a fistful, and eat them with bread as an after school snack. To this day, we all still love olives!

We had one *Fatima* who lived with us to help my mother with the household chores. ("Fatima" was the common name used for an Arab housekeeper.) With five young boys in the house, my mother would make sure our *Fatima* was old and homely so we wouldn't get any ideas! The *Fatima* would sleep on the floor, usually under the long dining table, which was the only available space.

Cooking was done on hot coals. Even bread was baked on hot coals. There were community ovens where you could pay to have your bread baked, and my mother would use them from time to time. However all the Jewish families would use these ovens on Friday for the weekly *Dafina*.

A *Dafina* is a traditional Sephardic Sabbath meal with eggs (cooked in the shell), rice, chick peas, meat and whatever else one might throw in the pot. The whole thing cooks from Friday at sundown to Saturday at noon. (I recently discovered that the tradition of the *Dafina* originated with Spanish Jews and is several hundred years old, dating back to before the Spanish Inquisition.) Though we rarely ate meat during the week, we always had meat in the weekly *Dafina*, though the quality of the meat would vary.

Each *Dafina* was designed for the needs of the family -- one egg per person, 2 small potatoes each, etc. You could therefore tell the size and/or wealth of a family by the size of their pot. Colored aluminum pots would be used, with the name or initials of the family written on the side for identification. As added insurance against unauthorized hands in the pot, the lid would be "glued" with some kind of paste made from dough. Broken seals would lead to big arguments with the oven attendants! Use of the communal oven for the *Dafina* had to be paid for in advance, since one is not supposed to handle money on the Sabbath. *Fatimas* would carry pots for two or three families at a time on a wooden tray on their heads.

On Saturday afternoon, the air around the oven would be thick with the distinctive, inviting smell of dozens of *Dafinas*. The pots would be spread out on the ground and each family would hunt for their pot. Occasionally, a family would get the wrong *Dafina*, but no one complained if it was good and plentiful!

The whole family would gather to eat meals together -- my parents and all eight kids (Renée was married and out of the house by this time). Our apartment at the Place de Verdun had a long hallway and our table was in the hallway, the only place it would fit. David's seat was at the head of the table, and the rest of us would usually sit in the same place out of habit. Sibling squabbles were kept to a minimum at the table since David would get up and leave if things got out of hand; he hated arguments. Claudia and my mother would also help keep the peace.

Though she was often the peacemaker, Claudia was also strong willed and would sometimes get caught up in the fray. She worked for a time at the French department store chain Les Galleries Lafayette in Casablanca. She was very generous and would always bring presents to the house from the store. Jacques recalls that the first watch he ever bought was at that store, to take advantage of her employee discount.

The apartment had four large rooms and a kitchen. My parents had their own bedroom, as did David. The three girls, Claudia, Esther and Marie, shared a bed in the third room. Marie being the smallest girl, would always be in the middle. They were constantly bickering over the smallest of things, which continued well into their adult lives. Marie and I were close since we are only two years apart in age. Still, we would fight and if I hit her, she would not stop crying for the rest of the day. She was very strong willed, *very* stubborn and thought she knew it all so she could not stand being corrected.

The fourth room was the living room, with a sofa that Jacques used as a bed. I usually slept on the floor next to Jacques, on a mattress or rug that I would pull out at night. André, never wanting to be a bother, would sleep wherever he could find a place. Maurice, the youngest, would often sleep with my parents, or wherever he could find an unused rug or mattress.

Jacques was a fitful sleeper, tossing, turning and jerking so much that he would often fall off the sofa without waking up. Seizing the opportunity, I would quickly take his place. Upon waking in the morning, he would be quite surprised to find himself on the floor and me on the sofa! It wasn't until all six of my older siblings were married and out of the house that I got to sleep in a real bed.

When visitors came from Rabat, my parents would give up their bed and the boys would be bumped down, although there's not much further to go when you're already sleeping on the floor!

We only had one toilet, a water closet or WC as it is commonly called in Europe. There was no toilet paper back then, so we used newspaper.

Every year a few days prior to Yom Kippur, my mother would buy one live chicken for each person, to be slaughtered the night before Yom Kippur in keeping with the Jewish tradition of offering a "sacrifice" to purge one of their sins.

Since we were short on extra room, the chickens were kept in the WC until they met their demise. There were roosters for the boys, and hens for the girls. The roosters would crow at all hours of the day and night. We would open the door and throw seed in to feed them, then shut the door quickly so they wouldn't escape. Trying to go to the bathroom with eleven live chickens in a small closet was daunting, to say the least.

After a couple of years of this, my father decided that something needed to be done, so he built a temporary coop on the balcony. Unfortunately, the roof design of this coop was weak and the chickens pecked their way through and out of the coop. Chickens can fly short distances and within minutes, they jumped up onto the railing and flew off the fifth floor balcony. For some, their freedom was short lived because they got caught in electrical wires. I don't recall if we were able to round up the rest of them, but I do recall my mother being quite vocal about losing expensive chickens!

The night before Yom Kippur, the neighborhood *Shohet* would go door to door, dangle a chicken above each person's head while saying a prayer, then slit the chicken's throat. Since our building housed only Jewish families, the *Shohet* would start on the first floor and work his way up. We would know he was getting closer to our apartment by the ever louder sound of the squawking chickens that were meeting their maker.

The *Shohet* would hold the chicken with his left hand like a violin -- with the upper part of the chicken's neck under his chin. With his right hand, he would slit the chicken's throat, like a bow across the violin. The "sacrifice" would take place in the kitchen, where two large basins were at the ready. One basin, right side up, was filled with sand to catch the blood. The other basin, upside down, was used to contain the headless but still moving chickens. This basin would bounce and clang for a few minutes until the chicken died, then would bounce again as another chicken was thrown under it. Once all the chickens had stopped moving, the feathering would begin, done by hired *Fatimas*. I will leave you to imagine the scene as eleven chickens were plucked in one place at one time.

Our prize possession was the short wave radio. During the war, my father would press his ear to the radio to listen to the London-based broadcasts of the French resistance, including speeches from General De Gaulle, which were barely audible over the static of the deliberate signal jamming by the Vichy government. His friends at the cafe would eagerly await the latest news, since they did not have short wave radios. My father loved politics and relished his role as "newscaster" to his friends.

Even with the financial hardship and lack of amenities, we had a lot of joy in the house. The radio brought us music from Spain, France and other European countries. My sisters would sing all the time, especially songs by Rina Ketty and Tino Rossi, and our home was filled with music and laughter. To this day, I love music from all over the world and so appreciate my IPod, with thousands of songs to choose from.

Chapter 5

I *loved* school and was an avid reader, poring over newspapers, magazines and books. I was captivated by the printed word, which connected me with a world much larger than my own, allowing me to experience politics and world events. I would get on my bike early each morning to get the first newspaper of the day, then would read it front to back with a passion. I felt like I was in the middle of a big, never ending story, a feeling which has lasted to this day.

I was also a dreamer and an adventurer, always eager to try something new. I would ride my bike up to thirty miles outside Casablanca so I could pick blackberries. I was about 13 years old when, upon my return from one of those trips, I got very sick with a high fever.

At the time there was an epidemic of typhoid fever throughout Morocco and I was diagnosed with the illness. Typhoid is characterized by long periods of high fever with no breaks. I was very sick and lost more than half of my body weight. With each passing day, my condition worsened.

Typhoid took a heavy toll on young and old alike, and several *Casablancais*, including some close friends, lost their lives from it. Understanding the urgency, my entire family was mobilized to take care of me. Since we did not own a refrigerator and ice was extremely important to lower my temperature, my oldest brother David would make the rounds of French bars near closing time so he could get ice to control the intense fever. For this, I owe my life to him and he continues to be my hero to this day.

I was indeed very lucky and after being bedridden for a month, I started feeling better. My main concern was that I had lost precious school time and would not be able to catch up. The teacher wrote my parents to say that since I had been an excellent student, my absence would not affect my grades and I would have no problem catching up to other students. This had quite an influence on my morale and helped me get better more rapidly since I could not wait to get back to school.

In school, I met Henri Elkouby who, to this day, is one of my best friends. Henri was quite versed in Hebrew, loved politics, and was a great student. We both graduated from Middle school with honors.

After graduation from the *Alliance*, my father enrolled me in the *École Industrielle et Commerciale* of Casablanca where my subjects were French, English, Accounting and Business Administration. France was at war with Germany and Italy in 1939 and all Italian students were expelled from school. There was a brilliant Italian student in my class who was always ranked #1 among the 42 students; I was second. When France entered WWII against Italy, he was expelled from school, which gave me the opportunity to become number one. However my perch at the top did not last long because upon the defeat of the French army in Europe in June 1940, the Vichy French, under Marshal Philippe Pétain, once again ruled Morocco and the Italian student returned to class.

Class Picture (I'm third from the left, bottom row), 1938

The Nazi victory over France in June 1940 put France's overseas colonies and protectorates under the control of the Vichy puppet regime in southern France. Sultan Mohammed V, who already was forced to approve the French colonial policies, now also came under pressure from the Germans via the Vichy regime. Like previous Sultans, he tried to protect his Jewish subjects, but under the Vichy regime, he had little room to maneuver.

In October 1940 and August 1941, the Vichy Government of France under Pétain enacted laws that discriminated against Moroccan Jews. It set quotas on the number of Jewish doctors and lawyers, ejected students from French schools and forced many Jews living in the European quarters to move to the *mellahs*. Mohammed V negotiated to limit the impact of the laws, but had no choice but to put his seal on them.

I was 16 when I received a letter explaining that because I was a Jew, I could no longer study at the École Industrielle. I was devastated because school was my *raison d'être*. Mohammed the Fifth, the Sultan of Morocco at the time, strongly objected to this unilateral decree and act of discrimination from the Vichy French. He insisted that Moroccan Jews were his protected subjects and were to be treated differently from the European Jews.

After long debates, two percent of Moroccan Jews were allowed to return to school. Being of good standing, I was among those allowed to return, as was my friend Joseph Bouzaglou, who was two years my senior. Nevertheless, it was difficult for us to continue our studies in that school because most of the teachers were anti-Semites and were frequently unfair to the Jewish students.

At 16 years old, 1941

During the period of 1941 to 1942, we experienced severe restrictions throughout Morocco. Basic items such as coal, flour, sugar, meat and clothing, were in short supply and extremely difficult to obtain, requiring hours of waiting in endless lines. My brother André, who was only 12 at the time, would volunteer to stand in line to get needed rations, particularly cooking coal. André was above the fray and never complained. He could always be counted on and did much for the family, with little recognition.

Water was also under severe restriction. For a time, the only way to get water was to carry it up to the apartment. André would repeatedly go up and down five flights of stairs with heavy jugs of water, filling the bathtub so we could have water for cooking and washing up. At other times, water was available from the faucet but only at certain times, usually at night. We would stay awake until the late hours so we could fill our basins and bathtub.

Because we did not know the exact water delivery time, we would keep the faucets open in order not miss the distribution. If we fell asleep and the water arrived, it would flood the apartment and spill through the rain holes in our balcony to the street below. When that happened, we would get fined for abuse of a precious resource.

Chapter 6

In 1941 after the German armies invaded several European countries, a large number of Jews arrived in Morocco to take refuge in our cities. For the most part, these refugees were educated men of some means, which they used in the crossing of France and Spain. Because the refugees had no place to stay, many Moroccan Jewish families took them in.

Among these refugees was a Jewish musician named Albert Karmazyn. Born in Warsaw, Poland, Albert arrived in Casablanca penniless, with nothing but his violin and several letters of awards and accomplishments from various cities in Europe, including first prize from the Paris Conservatory. Albert was 33 years old and played the violin beautifully, having studied with famous teachers in Paris and Strasbourg. I met Albert at a friend's house, where he was giving music lessons to my friend's brother -- I remember him kneeling on the floor, moving the boy's foot to show him the proper rhythm.

My mother was a very generous woman, so it did not take much convincing for her to offer our hospitality to Albert, and he was invited to live with us. This act of kindness ended up changing the course of the Chriqui family's destiny, as will be covered later.

When the day arrived for his move to our apartment, Albert showed up with two other refugee friends who also had no place to go. One, Joseph Aramov, was a painter, and the other, Gustav

Shmiliver, was a poet. My mother, bless her heart, said "No problem, we will find room for them." So we "adopted" all three.

Despite a lack of space and rationed food, we shared what little we had with them. Two of the refugees slept on the floor, next to the sofa. I was 16 years old and like a sponge, absorbing everything they had to say. We spent many nights talking into the wee hours about politics, war, and Jewish life in Europe, a continent I knew nothing about, as well as the families they had left behind. The three refugees we took in were quite educated and their presence was a great source of learning for me.

Albert Karmazyn, 1940's

Albert was a very resourceful man. To make a few francs he would sell pencils to local businesses. When Joseph Aramov left, I shared my floor space with Gustav Shmiliver. It was an experience I will never forget. Gustav was like an encyclopedia. He spoke several languages, and shared his many stories and experiences with me. So many of life's lessons I carry with me to this day, I learned from him. He also helped me with my new language, English, since he was fluent. I loved his poetic skills and his wonderful sense of humor.

Unfortunately, I never again saw Shmiliver or Aramov after they left us.

During the long evenings when the war was raging in Europe, Albert Karmazyn would entertain us with his violin. My brother Jacques, a *bon-vivant* and a great dancer, would invite his friends including Alberto Mahfoda, who was a wonderful flamenco singer. We would dance and laugh the night away. It provided us with free entertainment and helped us through the long curfew periods.

Alberto was from the Spanish zone of Morocco and though he spoke a little French, he could not write it. One time, he asked Jacques to write a letter for him to his French girlfriend. He asked Jacques to say that it was not his pen that was writing, but his heart. The girlfriend responded that it was neither Alberto's pen nor his heart that wrote the letter, but it was Jacques Chriqui!

Jacques, 1940's

When teams of German officers started arriving in Morocco after France's defeat in 1940, their first order of business was to track down the European Jewish refugees. They arrested our friends, including Albert, and placed them in an internment camp in the City of Azemmour, about sixty miles from Casablanca. My sister

Claudia, who was 22 at the time, would travel by bus to Azemmour to bring food packages to Albert, who informed her that he was waiting for a U.S. visa from a cousin who lived in Brooklyn, NY.

Albert and Claudia were great friends, and that friendship developed into love. Albert was very serious about marrying Claudia before his imminent immigration to the United States so that he could more easily have her join him later as his wife. My mother was completely against this marriage and would tell Albert, "*Makache l'Amerique*" (Arabic for "there is no way she will go to America"). Well they did get married in a civil ceremony, on the same day that my brother David married Viviane Elbaz. Mother was not happy about that wedding either, but agreed nonetheless to hold the two religious ceremonies in our home.

Claudia in her Henna dress, 1941

In late 1941 Albert Karmazyn left Morocco for the USA and Claudia stayed behind awaiting her own visa, which took several months to receive.

Chapter 7

I was 16 years old when I first saw Juliette Gabay at the local swimming pool, the Casablanca *Piscine Municipale*. I was immediately struck by her beauty and it was love at first sight. Juliette had fair skin, dark hair and a twinkle in her light blue eyes. All the neighborhood boys gathered around her, but I found a way to be introduced to her through a common friend. Juliette had a great sense of humor and a wonderful personality. She was also 16 while her younger sister and best friend Yvonne was 12.

The Gabay's lived in a first floor apartment on Boulevard de Bordeaux. Her father Leon Gabay, a very distinguished Maurice Chevalier look-a-like, came from a prominent family from Safi, 130 miles from Casablanca. Mr. Gabay held a high position at a local bank. He was a kind, generous man with a great sense of humor, very proud of his family of two daughters and one son, Henri.

Yvonne and Juliette Gabay as teenagers, 1940's

Both of Juliette's parents were orphans and heads of household with responsibilities towards their younger siblings when they were married at 21 years of age. Leon had four sisters and Rachel had three brothers. Leon's father was a rabbi from Safi and Juliette's mother Rachel was born into a prominent family, the Abittans of Casablanca, closely related to the well known Moreno family and the family of Rabbi Abraham Ifrah, Dean of Casablanca judges. Rachel was a great cook and when I was invited to lunch as Juliette's *petit ami* I enjoyed her superb cuisine and the warmth of this exceptional family.

Juliette at 18 years old, 1943

That was approximately the time when I wrote Juliette the first of many letters where I expressed my love and how much she meant to me. I could never have imagined then that she would keep that letter, along with over a hundred others that followed in the ensuing years. Discovering these letters after her passing is a tremendous gift, and a testimony of our deep mutual love for each other. Reading them now has also provided me with a treasure trove of information about my first years in America.

Chapter 8

By early 1942, things were getting worse for Jews in Morocco. The German Commission tasked the Vichy French to take a census of all Jewish families. We were asked to furnish detailed information about our household, including a complete list of our possessions, bank accounts, gold items and cash. I remember my brother Jacques filling out a form declaring that he owned two pairs of pants and two shirts.

Jews were not allowed to work for the city and many managerial jobs were also off limits. The daily newspapers, *Le Petit Marocain* and *La Vigie Marocaine* would post job announcements which stated that Jews need not apply.

Large signs were posted throughout Casablanca that said "Jews, November 15th is your day". At the time, we didn't know what would happen on that day though we understood it was something bad. This uncertainty weighed heavily on all the Moroccan Jews. We had heard news accounts that Jews were being rounded up in Europe and we feared that this would be our fate as well. I now know that Nov 15th was the date when all Jews were to be arrested and deported to European extermination camps.

Shortly before November 15th, 1942 Claudia received her immigration papers so she could now join her husband Albert in the United States. She boarded the Portuguese ship *Serpa Pinto,* the last ship to leave Casablanca for the U.S. until the waning years of the war. I imagine that on the month-long journey to New York, the *Sherpa Pinto* must have travelled through waters infested with German subs and crossed paths with a large armada of allied ships en route to Morocco.

In 1942, WWII operations against Germany were not going very well for the Allies. Germany was successfully advancing deep inside the Soviet Union and, with its invasion of that territory, was poised to capture the rich Caucasian oil fields. At the same time, the British 7th Army in Libya had serious difficulties confronting the Africa Corps of Rommel and had suffered heavy losses in its attempt to stop the advance of Rommel's army toward Egypt and the Suez Canal. The American forces who entered the war were not only unprepared, but were also busy fighting the Japanese in the Pacific. The important sea lanes of the Atlantic were under constant attack by German U-boats and ship losses were heavy. It was vital during high level conferences between the Big 3 (Roosevelt, Churchill and Stalin) that the U.S. and England quickly open a second front in order to change the course of events, acquire a strategic advantage, divert German forces and relieve pressure in critical areas in Europe and Africa.

Operation Torch, designed by Churchill and Roosevelt, called for amphibious landings in North Africa, mainly in Morocco and Algeria, which at the time were territories under control of Vichy France. It called for a major U.S. deployment and was to be the U.S.'s first major offensive since WWI.

The task was of monumental proportion. No navy had ever transported thousands of men, weapons, ammunition and supplies, to another continent over 3,000 miles away, across hostile waters. American General Dwight D. Eisenhower was put in charge of Operation Torch. Eisenhower, in less than a year, had risen from obscurity as a staff colonel in Texas, to command his country's largest combined operation. It was to involve ten Divisions, a huge armada of British and US ships, and dozens of planes for an aerial assault.

Three task forces were to strike simultaneously: at Casablanca in Morocco, and at Oran and Algiers in Algeria. The landings took place on November 8, 1942, just one week before the November 15th "deadline". In Morocco, the American Naval forces were led by General George S. Patton. His objective was to land in the port of Casablanca, however the city was too strongly defended, so the American assaults were made on the beaches of Fedala, Port Lyautey and Safi instead. It was a time of dramatic moments and an extraordinary seesaw of events.

I was an eyewitness to the attack on Casablanca. My building was very close to the harbor and from our apartment on the fifth floor we had a bird's eye view of the entire battle. I was about 17 years old and it was an experience I will never forget.

I woke up that morning to the sound of big guns. The Vichy French had declined an earlier opportunity to surrender, so the Americans and British attacked from the sea and the air. The ocean was black with the great number of transport ships. From our balcony it was a spectacular view, as we watched allied planes dive and bomb the Vichy ships that were trying to get out of the harbor. We were so fascinated by what we were watching that it never occurred to us that we could be in danger from a bomb going astray, which did happen in other parts of the city. One French battle ship, the *Jean Bart* with its 15mm guns, was shooting from the harbor and the noise was deafening.

As the battle was taking place in the harbor, American planes were dropping thousands of leaflets on Casablanca. The leaflets, in both French and Arabic, contained a message from President Roosevelt that said the Americans were there to liberate us from German occupation, that they would do us no harm, and they would leave once the threat from Italy and Germany was removed. The message requested that we not stand in their way so that peace could return to the region. The leaflet was signed by Dwight D. Eisenhower, then Lieutenant General and Commander in Chief of the American Forces. My brother André, just 13 years old at the time, kept one of the leaflets and still has it to this day (see next page).

Message du Président des Etats Unis

Le Président des Etats Unis m'a chargé comme Général Commandant en Chef des Forces Expéditionnaires Américaines de faire parvenir aux peuples de l'Afrique française du Nord le message suivant:

Aucune nation n'est plus intimement liée, tant par l'histoire que par l'amitié profonde, au peuple de France et à ses amis que ne le sont les Etats Unis d'Amérique.

Les Américains luttent actuellement, non seulement pour assurer leur avenir, mais pour restituer les libertés et les principes démocratiques de tous ceux qui ont vécu sous le drapeau tricolore.

Nous venons chez vous pour vous libérer des conquérants qui ne désirent que vous priver à tout jamais de vos droits souverains, de votre droit à la liberté du culte, de votre droit de mener votre train de vie en paix.

Nous venons chez vous uniquement pour anéantir vos ennemis — nous ne voulons pas vous faire de mal.

Nous venons chez vous en vous assurant que nous partirons dès que la menace de l'Allemagne et de l'Italie aura été dissipée.

Je fais appel à votre sens des réalités ainsi qu'à votre idéalisme.

Ne faites rien pour entraver l'accomplissement de ce grand dessein.

Aidez-nous, et l'avènement du jour de la paix universelle sera hâté.

DWIGHT D. EISENHOWER
Lieutenant Général, Commandant en Chef
des Forces Expéditionnaires Américaines.

In the end, the Vichy French gave up the fight and later, to our great satisfaction, they joined the Allied forces in their fight against Germany and Italy.

Because they landed miles away, it took the American soldiers a few days to make their way to Casablanca. We had been following the developments on the radio, so we knew that soldiers would soon be entering the city. I was very excited, believing that the American presence would change the course of the country for the better.

A large crowd of people, Jews, Arabs, Europeans, gathered in the Place de France, the city's central square, to await their arrival. We had never seen Americans so there was tremendous curiosity and a mood of anticipation.

The first thing we saw was a jeep with four soldiers, sent ahead to make sure there were no hostiles in the square. Then slowly but surely, the foot soldiers arrived from all directions.

For days I had thought about what they would look like, envisioning soldiers in crisp uniforms, walking in unison in a kind of grand military parade. Instead, the soldiers were bedraggled, muddy, unshaven and exhausted, dragging their feet like prisoners in a chain gang. To me, they looked like giants -- big, burly and tall. The crowd's reaction was mixed -- some were happy, others were wary, and many didn't know what to think. But the soldiers came in with smiles, waving and handing out chocolates and gum. One soldier, who had no candy, gave me his empty wallet instead. Moments later, another boy ran up to me and snatched it from my hands.

Though some newspaper articles spoke of the American's "invading" Morocco, the Jews greeted the Americans with an open heart and welcomed their presence. Even without fully knowing what would have happened on November 15th, we understood that the Americans had saved us from a terrible fate.

Chapter 9

After the landings, it was difficult for the U.S. Army to find Moroccan citizens who could speak English, Arabic and French, so they relied on young men fresh from school who had some language skills.

I was barely 17 years old when I got a job with the U.S. Army Contracting Office. Shortly after, I was transferred to the Civilian Personnel Office of the Air Transport Command or ATC (there was no U.S. Air Force at the time) which was recruiting a large number of local personnel for assignment to various bases. We were hiring Arabs, French, Spanish and Portuguese workers, and every morning a large crowd of job seekers would gather outside the ATC personnel office at Camp Cazes, just outside Casablanca. Together with an American Officer, I would stand in the middle of a very large circle of job seekers, all anxious to work for the Americans. My job was to assist in the selection process by using my knowledge of Arabic and French. We repeated this process daily for many months until we hired thousands of local workers to support the military at our base and others in Morocco.

First job with US Army at 17 years old, 1942

Prior to working for the Americans, I had always gone by my given name, Salomon. But the Americans found it difficult, so I became Sidney, and have been so ever since.

Americans had a more open, casual way of social interaction than the more formal French. They also didn't have the class distinctions the French had. A French acquaintance would never say, "Hey Sid, how's the family?", something so common and ordinary among the Americans. This more casual interaction was foreign to me at first, but I took to it immediately.

In 1943 I was assigned to the U.S. Army Judge Advocate Office. That Office was responsible for the investigation of local accidents and/or crimes involving American soldiers. My job consisted of coordinating with the French or Arabic courts when local residents were involved as victims and/or witnesses. I translated French and Arabic documents into English, and vice versa, and served as a sworn interpreter for the Army Court Martials.

I vividly remember a particular case where an American Military Police sergeant was accused of raping an 18 year old Jewish girl. The girl had accepted a ride to her job on the base but instead of taking her to the base, the sergeant had driven to a deserted beach where he had raped her at gunpoint.

Afterwards, the girl went to the American Hospital to be examined and as a result, the soldier was charged. A General Court Martial was established to try the soldier. I interpreted the entire case, which was somewhat embarrassing at my young age, particularly because I knew the girl. The soldier was found guilty and given a prison sentence.

These tribunals were held at the Anfa Hotel in a suburb of Casablanca. In that same hotel and in that very same room where the above mentioned trial took place, a conference of world importance was held in 1943: the historic Casablanca Conference between U.S. President Franklin Delano Roosevelt and British Prime Minister Winston Churchill. In that conference a joint declaration pledged that the war would end only with the unconditional surrender of the axis states (Germany, Japan and Italy).

Pictures from mid 1940's

Joe Bouzaglou's jeep, purchased from the U.S. Govt, 1945

At Camp Cazes, 1944

At 20 years old, 1945

Chapter 10

Life in Casablanca improved after the landings, but many critical items were still hard to find. Clothing for instance was very scarce and we often relied on the U.S. Merchant Marine whose members sold us most of their clothes when they visited the city. Because I was employed by the U.S. Army, I was entitled to special weekly rations of sugar, rice, flour, soap and fabrics. This last item was particularly appreciated by my sisters Esther and Marie at the time of their weddings since they needed new clothes.

Around that time, big packages of goodies started arriving from America. Our sister Claudia, now living in New York, was spending much of her hard earned dollars to buy and send us critical food and clothing packages on a regular basis.

I was fortunate to have great friends such as Henri Leb, Roger Harroch, Edouard Bendahan, Maurice Perez, Albert Assayag, Albert Nahon, Paul Harroch, Sammy Oiknine, Joe Bouzaglou, Henry Sibony and Henri Elkouby. I remained close with these childhood friends throughout my life and am still close with Henri Leb and Henri Elkouby to this day. Humor was extremely important and we all learned early not to take things too seriously. Each one in my group of friends would tell jokes and try to top the other in who could get the biggest laugh. The laughter was infectious.

We loved everything about America -- the food, clothes, music and singers. We learned how to dance the jitterbug, swings, rumbas etc. Each week, we would stage "surprise" parties in a different home, called such because everyone needed to bring a small "surprise", like a bottle of wine or something to eat.

When the parties were at my house, the living room and one of the adjacent bedroom (separated from the living room by French doors) would be the dance floor. My father would help me completely dismantle the bed to get it out of the way, then he and my mother would sit by the door waiting for my guests to arrive.

Our parties were always held in the afternoons because good Jewish girls did not go out at night. We all knew the lyrics of famous WWII era songs by Frank Sinatra, Bing Crosby, the Andréw sisters etc. For music, we had old 78 rpm records and phonographs with changeable needles. Only later were we were introduced to 33 rpm records when an American friend got them from the base theater.

I would always tango with my preferred partner, Juliette Gabay. My love for Juliette was growing and I frequently took the lead in organizing these parties just so I could dance with Juliette.

Juliette was very hard to read -- I surmised that she liked being with me because she always accepted my invitations, but she was not demonstrative in any way, which was typical for the girls at that time. It was not proper to show any affection without some kind of commitment.

I knew many soldiers from my work on the American base and soon discovered that some of them were good musicians. I invited a few to play for a group of friends, which was the beginning of a close collaboration. They formed a dynamic 5-piece band and would practice by playing for us every weekend. We would reciprocate with the best we could offer in food and wine. To our delight, they played all the American tunes we loved, and that I was so familiar with, having heard them on the American radio broadcast on the base, the ABS (Atlantic Base Section).

Chapter 11

In 1944, we celebrated two weddings at home. My sister Esther wed Elie Elbaz, a calm and distinguished gentleman who worked as a cashier at the same company as Esther. Marie married a handsome and charming man named Maurice Ohana. We knew Maurice very well since he was a close friend of my brother Jacques. We considered Maurice as our brother because his own family lived far away in Safi. After their weddings, both couples lived in our apartment because housing was very difficult to find and their financial means were limited. Elie and Maurice were wonderful additions to the family and we loved them both dearly.

Both couples had children at about the same time. Esther and Elie's first born was Albert (we nicknamed him Bebert) and Maurice and Marie's first born was Lucienne, whom we called Lullu. A second child for the Ohana family, Roger, was born in February 1948 just one day after Suzanne was born to the Elbazes.

Maurice Ohana and Marie, 1940's

By 1948, Marie and her family had moved to their own apartment; Esther and Elie were still living with us. Marie's sister in law, Mrs. Murciano, was a midwife so four of Marie's children, Lucienne, Roger, Henry and Corinne were born at home.

When Suzanne was born, I was 22 years old. I took charge of getting my sister Esther to the hospital, which included practically carrying her down the five flights of stairs. It was the middle of the night and Elie was an emotional wreck and didn't know what to do. We had no transportation so I flagged down the only passing car and begged the driver to take us to the hospital. In my haste to get Esther to the hospital, I left Elie behind. By the time he arrived at the hospital, Suzanne had already entered the world and Elie was overcome with joy at the news that he was now the father of a beautiful baby girl.

In 1945, we celebrated the marriage of my brother Jacques to Solange Amiel, whom Jacques had met at one of my parties in our parent's home. Solange was a beautiful woman with fair skin, smiling blue eyes and a great personality. They were married in February, and the only lodging they could find at the time was a tiny apartment on the roof of a centrally located building.

Their first child, Lydia, was born in November 1945. When she was 8 or 9 months old, Lydia became ill with a serious case of pneumonia. Both lungs were affected and the constant use of oxygen did not help much. The entire family was extremely concerned about Lydia as her breathing worsened by the day.

Twice a day Lydia was visited by a local doctor, who was not optimistic about her condition. He indicated that Lydia's case was serious and that he had tried everything, with no success. He mentioned that he had heard about a very new medicine called Penicillin which could possibly help her. Such medicine, however, was not available in Morocco, except possibly at the American Hospital.

When I learned of this, I reported the matter to my boss, U.S. Army Captain Joseph Goldfarb. Captain Goldfarb listened to my story, put on his hat and left the room. He returned with a small vial. Time being of the essence, he offered me his car and driver to rush the medicine to Jacques' house.

Lydia Chriqui, 1946

That same day, Lydia was given 2 shots of Penicillin. The next day there was a definite improvement in her condition, and it became clear that the danger had passed. It was as if my beautiful niece was saved by divine intervention. Another gravely ill baby was also saved with the remaining portion of that miraculous medicine. To this day, Lydia is like a daughter to me. Lydia currently lives in Paris, France.

Chapter 12

By the beginning of 1947 most of the American troops had left Morocco for duties in Europe. I was transferred to the last remaining American outfit called the US. Army Grave Registration Service, where I worked as a case coordinator. It was heartbreaking to see so many young soldiers who had been killed in the North African theater of operations, being shipped back to the U.S. in coffins.

Throughout 1947 I was consumed with thoughts of immigrating to the United States. My sister Claudia, who by now was living in California, had prepared two affidavits of support on my behalf, which were required by immigration laws. Albert and she were very anxious to have me join them. I was 22, spoke English well, and my dream was to live in America.

In early 1948, I was issued an immigration visa by the U.S. Consulate of Casablanca. I had mixed feelings when I received that precious document. On the one hand, I was happy to be the first Jewish Moroccan young man in my circle of friends and family to leave Morocco for the United States after WWII. But on the other hand, I was quite sad to leave my sweetheart behind. Juliette was of marrying age and I was afraid I would lose her by going so far away. We were great friends and we loved being together, but there was no marriage commitment since I was unemployed and contemplating a new life in the U.S. We decided it was best for my future that I not miss this wonderful opportunity, and that destiny would work its course. If we were meant to be together, the separation would be a good test for both of us. She did not commit herself to me, nor did I to her.

Prior to travelling to the US, I had never ventured outside Morocco. In fact, I had never gone further than 100 miles from Casablanca. I was planning to travel by ship to Marseille, take a train to Paris then to Le Havre, where I would board another ship for the trans Atlantic voyage to New York. From there, I was to travel by train to Chicago, then take another train to California. I was quite excited to see all these places but as the departure date approached, I was saddened at the thought of leaving my family, my friends and particularly Juliette.

The much anticipated day finally arrived: May 1st 1948. My entire family, several close friends, Juliette and her sister Yvonne accompanied me to the harbor. The emotions were high and I felt like a little bird leaving the nest for the unknown.

My mother Simha, 1947

Together with my friend Albert Assayag, who accompanied me to France where he was to vacation, we were to clear French Customs in Casablanca. The policy for travelers at the time was that you could not carry foreign currency. Aware of these restrictions, we hid dollar bills inside a suitcase's handle and fooled the *gendarmes* (policemen).

We embarked on the *Koutoubia*, a French ship bound for Marseille. It finally dawned on me that I was leaving my neighborhood, my family, my home, my friends, my sweetheart and all the precious moments I had spent with all of them. As the *Koutoubia* was leaving the harbor toward higher seas, and while I could still see the Casablanca coastline, my heart was full of sadness and nostalgia of the music and passion of a country where I had been happy. All the pictures of my life, the smells, the sounds, the feelings were going through my mind. I closed my eyes so I could savor the moment of these souvenirs. It was my entire youth I was leaving behind.

To save money, Albert and I slept in the galleys (fourth class) which was mostly occupied by Senegalese soldiers returning to France after their service in Morocco. The food and general living conditions in the galleys were deplorable. From the first night at sea, I was seasick and homesick, and was having second thoughts about going to such a faraway place.

Albert and I would visit other parts of the ship, and would bribe the Senegalese soldiers with our ration of wine and bread and perhaps a few francs so they would watch our belongings during our absences. In the evenings, we would dress in our fanciest suits and climb up several stories on ladders to sneak into the ship's first class, where we had plenty of fun dancing with French women and enjoying the nightly shows. Two famous singers, Tino Rossi and Lilly Fayol, were on that ship and treated us to some of their hit songs.

The crossing took three days and during those days I started a regular and detailed correspondence with Juliette describing what I was experiencing. Other letters would follow throughout my journey in Europe and my years in the United States. I rediscovered these letters after she passed in 2008. Here are excerpts from one of my first letters to Juliette (translated from French):

May 2, 1948

Dearest Juliette:

Today is Sunday, the second day at sea. We will be arriving in Marseille tomorrow. Although the sea was rough yesterday, it is much calmer today. We sailed through the straits of Gibraltar and are now near the coast of Spain, close to the Baleares islands. I already miss you terribly and have been thinking of you constantly since I left Casablanca. I could not sleep the first night, asking myself why I ventured out on this long and lonely journey, leaving behind those I love so much? Frankly Juliette, we don't fully realize the attachment and love we have for someone until we go far away, especially when we know the absence will be a long one. I dreaded this moment and now I know how difficult it will be for me for the months and years to come.

True we were great friends and true there was nothing serious between us, but deep inside, ever since I was 16 my love for you has been growing. You are a part of me and I love you very much. I love your family and pray Hashem to unite us one day. I never knew I would be this emotional but I am writing this letter from my heart. Please write to me as I very much need to hear from you.

Your friend who cares so much about you.

Sidney

Chapter 13

The *Koutoubia* arrived in Marseille early May 3rd, 1948 and we set foot on French soil for the first time. We knew a lot about France from our school years, but we had never visited. After collecting our luggage, Albert stood watch over the bags while I arranged our train tickets to Paris. As he was standing near our luggage, a man came running by and stole one of my suitcases, the one where I had hidden the dollar bills. Albert quickly ran after him, knocked him to the ground, and retrieved the suitcase. We only stayed in Marseille long enough to get our train tickets, then we were off to Paris.

We arrived in Paris early the next morning. We immediately loved this unique and beautiful city. We rendezvoused with Paul Harroch, a mutual friend from Casablanca who now lived in Paris. Paul was kind enough to offer us lodging in his apartment. We visited many places and on the 7th of May 1948 I wrote the following to Juliette, giving her my first impressions of Paris.

Dearest Juliette,

I want to tell you how much I appreciated your visit to my parents on "Mimouna" [1] *night. It certainly was a very sweet thing on your part, especially when they are so sad after my departure. Again, I want to tell you how much you mean to me and how much I miss you. You are continuously on my mind.*

Paris is a beautiful city and our visits to the monuments, museums and theaters are a joy. Paul Harroch is most gracious; he wants us to visit the entire city, which is difficult to do in the few days I have here. The city is huge and to travel from one place to another we use the metro and buses. Although WWII has been over for the past three years, many essential things are still scarce here. Bread is rationed and to be served bread in a restaurant you need to buy coupons which restrict you to one small roll per meal. We brought with us from Morocco many cans of sardines which we have been trading to get our laundry and ironing done.

Yesterday we visited the "Musee Grevin" (a wax museum) where we experienced the Paris of yesterday and today through more astounding scenes and more than 100 life-size, three-dimensional models of the people who made headlines in French and world history. Then we visited the Mirage of Mirrors department where you are transported to another world of sculptures and miraculous places. We also visited the Eiffel Tower and enjoyed a panoramic view of this magnificent city. As you know I love music so we visited the Olympia where we were treated

---

[1] Mimouna is the last night of Passover when Jewish families prepare a table of pastries, and people visit one another.

to the great Bandoneon sound of an Argentinean orchestra with tango dancers, then to an American jazz band with Sidney Bechet. It was great. We visited the Trocadero and the Musee de l'Homme where you see skeletons of prehistoric men. The L'Arc de Triomphe and the Fontainebleau zoo is scheduled for tomorrow.

There are so many places to visit! My heart however is somewhere else. I wish so much you could be here with me enjoying all these beautiful places. I will be leaving Paris in 3 days by train to Le Havre in the Northern part of France, where I will be boarding the French Liner De Grasse for New York. I will be writing to you from there. I love you very much.

Sidney

I arrived in Le Havre on May 11th 1948 and embarked on the *De Grasse* for the transatlantic journey. The *De Grasse* had been commandeered by the Germans during the war as an accommodation ship. Before the Nazis retreated in 1944, they sank the ship with a depth charge. In 1945 the French Company *Generale Transatlantique*, which owned the ship, raised it from the water and had it refurbished. Beneath the passenger decks was a significant prize of war: a black Mercedes with a reinforced body and bullet proof glass which had once belonged to Adolph Hitler. The 3 1/2 ton vehicle was now the property of the French Government.

We sailed from Le Havre to Southampton, England, where we picked up more passengers, then sailed across the Atlantic to Halifax, Canada. It took us nine days to reach Halifax and it was quite an experience to visit my first city in the New World. Nicknamed the "city of trees", Halifax was a cosmopolitan city of sophisticated charm, and was elegant and lively. I loved the way it combined different architectural styles -- the stark lines of modern buildings and the 18th and 19th century buildings. I spent one day visiting Halifax then left at nighttime for New York.

De Grasse ship(above), on the ship's deck (below), 1948

I could hardly sleep, knowing I was just hours away from realizing my childhood dream. Finally I would be privileged to see America with my own eyes.

Moroccan Passport, 1948

PART TWO

UNITED STATES 1948 - 1949

Chapter 14

On the morning on May 22nd, 1948 the *De Grasse* entered the New York harbor on the Hudson River. Wide eyed with excitement, I watched the most spectacular view I had ever seen! Skyscrapers, bridges, ships, all symbols of American ingenuity. I was fascinated... it was so real and powerful, and so much more than I expected. My long wait was over. The America of my dreams was right in front of me. I was crying, my emotions high. My description of the arrival and my first steps in New York are described in the following letter to Juliette.

New York the 24th of May 1948

Dear Juliette,

Here I am in New York. The Atlantic crossing was a little rough, but I was not sick. Morocco seems so far away. The "De Grasse" slowly sailed toward Pier 88 where we disembarked. I, with my proficient English, was one of the first ones off the boat, and was pleasantly surprised at the politeness and professionalism of the immigration officials. They certainly weren't like that in Morocco!

At the pier there were a lot of people waiting for their immigrant relatives. Albert Karmazyn's cousin Esther Koch was to meet me, but in the middle of so many people it was difficult to find each other, particularly since we had never met. I heard my name being called on a loud speaker and we soon found each other. Esther is a small lady, pretty and very articulate. We were both very happy to see each other, and after recovering my luggage, we got in her car for travel to Brooklyn. It took one hour before we arrived at the Koch's home in the Jewish quarter. I phoned Claudia and it was quite emotional to hear her voice after six long years.

I had my first American meal on Saturday at noon: fish, green beans, cold chicken and very little bread. What a long way from our usual Dafina! They also had cold milk on the table, which seems to be a staple at every meal. It's amazing how much cold milk they drink here!

In the afternoon, Mr. Koch took me sightseeing. They have a train called the subway that goes underground, including under the Hudson river! What a sight awaited us when we emerged onto the street -- skyscrapers everywhere, high end stores, luxurious cars -there was so much to see I didn't know where to look! It seems like everything God ever created is in this town. I saw apples and pears as big as melons. I visited a store called Macy's, which is in a building that is 50 stories tall!. The store has a moving staircase called an escalator, and the elevators can carry dozens of people. I visited an immense theatre called Radio City Music Hall, and the Waldorf Astoria Hotel, one of the biggest and finest in the city.

That night, Mr. Koch brought me to a party. I was well received, and was the novelty in the room. Many didn't know where Morocco was, but they all thought I spoke English well and would have no trouble living in America.

As I'm writing this, I'm listing to some Arabic 78rpm records that I brought with me. The Koch's find this music very strange, but it reminds me of home.

Sidney

The Koch's lived in a Jewish neighborhood and kosher products and Hebrew newspapers were readily available, which had not been the case in Casablanca. Israel had just been formed and I was amazed to see the new Israeli flag flying outside the Waldorf Astoria Hotel.

A telephone was a luxury item in Morocco, yet it seemed like everyone in New York had one. I sent a telegram to Morocco and to Claudia so everyone would know I had arrived safely. To my astonishment, within five minutes of sending the telegram, Claudia called to tell me she had received it! I was mute with amazement at how quickly my message had been sent across thousands of miles. I told her I was planning to fly to California, but she encouraged me to take the train instead because planes were too dangerous.

I spent three or four days in New York, in complete awe at the grandeur and abundance of it all. I had never before seen the things that are so common in New York -- skyscrapers, suspension bridges, department stores and markets brimming with merchandise, luxurious cars, the subway, gridlock traffic.

One of the things that struck me the most was the clothes. People were very well dressed. Even my best suit was shabby in comparison. Elegant clothes made from beautiful fabrics were in every department store window, which was quite a change from Casablanca where our stores had been empty. Not only had clothing been scarce in Morocco, what was available was often made from a heavy, canvas-like material. And the shoes! I had never seen so many styles. I was overwhelmed by the wealth of this finery, though it seemed you needed wealth to buy any of it. Everything was very expensive to me since I did not realize that people's incomes here were larger than what I was used to.

I had promised Juliette that I would send her a bathing suit from America. Today that may seem like an odd request but back then, the available bathing suits were made from thick yarn that would get heavy when wet and stretch completely out of shape. There were so many beautiful ones to choose from, but Mrs. Koch told me the selection in Los Angeles would be even better so I decided to wait until I arrived in California to fulfill the promise.

Chapter 15

While in New York, I contacted my former boss, Captain Joseph Goldfarb, legal staff officer for the Air Transport Command in Morocco. This man was very special to me and to the entire Chriqui family because he was the one who had furnished the Penicillin that saved my niece Lydia and another baby in 1945. He was so happy to know that I was in his city and asked that I reserve the next day for him to take me around town. After a day of sightseeing, I spent Friday evening at his parents' home (his father was a well known Rabbi in Brooklyn) where we had an interesting conversation about Jewish life in Morocco, and how our Sephardic traditions differed from their Ashkenazi ones.

After the dinner, Joseph and I rode the subway together for a few stops. He was headed home and I was returning to the Koch's house. I asked if he knew the whereabouts of the other American captain from our office in Casablanca, Powell Wartel. Joseph said he had not been in direct contact with Powell, but knew he was a practicing attorney in New York, and that I could look him up in the lawyer directory at the library. We arrived at DeKalb station where Joseph hugged me, told me to stay in touch, and wished me well in California. I had four or five more stops to get to my destination.

After Joseph left, something inexplicable happened. I was sitting in the subway car facing the doors, thinking about Powell and how much I'd like to see him. At the next station, the subway stopped, people exited and one person entered right in front of me. That person was Powell Wartel. Our eyes met and he was as astonished as I was. I wondered for a moment if I was dreaming. "Is that really you, Sid?", Powell said.

To this day, I cannot explain how a person could possibly show up in front of you in a city of ten million people, at the exact moment that you are thinking about them.

* * * * * * * * * *

My journey to California was to take me through Chicago, then onto Los Angeles. The train from New York arrived in Chicago several hours late, so I missed my connection. I was informed that the next cross country train would not leave until the following day. I was upset about the delay, until I found out that the westbound train I missed had derailed around New Mexico, killing 17 people.

While in Chicago, I spent the day looking at all the wonderful things in the department stores. I was still astounded at the abundance of clothing and shoes available, after the years of privation in Casablanca. But everything was so expensive -- $5 for a shirt and $85 for a suit. Still keeping my eyes open for a bathing suit for Juliette, I splurged $19 and bought a beautiful one in the new, stretchy fabric that didn't exist in Morocco. Juliette would later tell me that it was a big hit at the local pool in Casablanca, where no one else had anything like it.

Chapter 16

The train to California was the "El Capitan", a modern train with sleepers that would unfold at the touch of a button. The journey from Chicago took 2 days and 2 nights through vast expanses of uninhabited countryside. I had already come so far, yet this part of the trip seemed interminable, as if I was travelling to the ends of the earth. I thought about Morocco and all that I had left behind and again wondered if I'd made the right decision. I wrote letters and chatted with fellow passengers to pass the time.

I finally arrived in Los Angeles where Claudia was waiting for me at the station. We cried tears of joy at seeing each other for the first time in almost 6 years. I clearly remember thinking in those first moments how much Claudia looked like André. She told me I was very thin but would have no problem putting on weight because people here ate like ogres.

Claudia and Albert had lived in New York their first few years together in America. He was in the Navy and she worked as a seamstress, a common job for immigrant women at that time. Claudia spoke no English and didn't know how to sew, but she quickly learned both, having little choice since Albert would be away for months at a time.

Albert played violin in the Navy orchestra and his discharge from the Navy occurred around the time the orchestra was touring the West Coast. He loved Los Angeles so much that he ended up staying and had Claudia join him.

Housing was affordable in the San Fernando Valley, which was very rural, comprised mostly of cattle farms and orange orchards. In 1947, with a low-cost mortgage obtained under the GI Bill, they purchased a small house for $12,000 at 10663 Valleyheart Drive in North Hollywood (now Universal City). That same year, their first son Allen was born. Claudia's house had all the modern appliances of the time including a stove, a refrigerator, and a washing machine, none of which my family had in Casablanca. Albert loved to cook and was into natural foods at a time when few people understood or cared about the effects of food on health.

The first few days were spent sightseeing -- the Hollywood Bowl, Sunset Blvd, Santa Monica Beach, site of expensive dance halls where drinks were $5, an exorbitant amount in my eyes. Albert took me to a film studio where the audience could watch movie auditions -- I got to see Mickey Rooney do a few scenes, which was very exciting. I also went shopping, buying things that were unavailable in Casablanca to send to my mother. Like in New York, there were beautiful clothes in the stores but unlike New York, the people in the streets were dressed in what I considered work clothes, what we know today as blue jeans. I couldn't understand why girls wore rolled up jeans when there were such beautiful dresses available.

Albert played the violin with the Los Angeles Philharmonic Orchestra, a job he held for forty years. For the first few weeks after my arrival, I accompanied him to performances as his "porter", carrying his violin through the employee entrance so I could sneak in without a ticket. Once inside, I would use my small binoculars to scope out an unoccupied seat.

The orchestra played concerts at the Hollywood Bowl and would also provide live music for stage shows. One of those shows, the musical "Annie, Get Your Gun" with Ethel Merman, was sold out for months. So Albert set up a chair for me in the corner of the orchestra pit, where I craned my neck for hours to watch the show. At the end when all the musicians stood up to be acknowledged by the audience I didn't know what to do, so I also stood up and bowed.

I developed a great appreciation for classical music from listening to Albert rehearse and perform, and from his large collection of 33's, which I inherited after his passing.

Claudia worked as a seamstress in downtown Los Angeles, now quite proficient in the trade after her years in New York. The shop where she worked had dozens of seamstresses but she was the fastest and thus was paid a higher wage than the others. Still, the Karmazyns struggled to make ends meet. Resourceful Albert made extra money on the side selling cemetery plots for the Sinai Mortuary for $150 each. Today, these plots are well over $10,000 each.

Chapter 17

Los Angeles was the land of plenty. You could get dozens of flavors of ice cream for just 5 cents a serving. Food was plentiful and I developed a taste for fruit juice, which we did not have in Morocco. In fact, everything was plentiful and within days of arriving, I was already itching to find a job.

The Karmazyns' house was near Universal Studios. I managed to sneak in one day and boldly ask for a job. Alas, since I was not an actor and knew nothing about film production, I obviously did not get hired.

It didn't take long to figure out that I would first need a car to get around. From the Valley to Hollywood and Downtown was far and there was little in the way of public transportation. During the war, American car production had stopped, so 1948 was the first year that new car models were available. Many were trading in their old cars for new ones, including Albert. While working for the Americans in Morocco, I had used the military post to send money so I would have a small sum when I arrived. It totaled $250, which I used to buy Albert's old car: a 1935 Chevy coupe, 2 seater with a running board, a long stick shift between the seats, and a kind of platform behind the seats.

My 1935 Chevy in North Hollywood, 1948

Now that I had a car, I was eager to explore the nightlife. So I went to the biggest dance hall in town, the Hollywood Palladium. This dance hall was like nothing I had ever seen. It was huge, with what seemed like a hundred member orchestra. I asked a girl to dance and she said no. I asked another girl and she also said no. After the third girl turned me down, I figured I was doing something wrong. So I asked a young man why no one would dance with me, and he said it wasn't proper unless I was first introduced. It turned out that his girlfriend had a sister, so he introduced her to me and I spent the rest of the evening dancing with her.

When it was time to go, I asked if I could drive her home and she said yes, but that she lived far away. "No problem", I said. There were no freeways at the time, and I had just been in Los Angeles about a week and had no idea where anything was. But I was feeling invincible with my car and new found friend, so she pointed me in the right direction and we drove off.....and kept driving.....and driving. She said something about Anaheim, which had no meaning to me. I eventually realized that she lived VERY FAR away, and any thoughts I may have had about what would happen when we got to her house quickly evaporated. When we finally arrived almost 2 hours later, I was so frustrated that I practically pushed her out of the car.

I started driving back the way I came, but didn't really know where I was going. Then the fog rolled in, obscuring the unfamiliar streets, and I was completely lost. By this time, it was one or two in the morning, and I had no idea where I was. So I stopped the car, got out, and waited for a passing motorist, which took awhile at that hour. I eventually flagged down another driver and asked how to get to North Hollywood. "North Hollywood is MILES from here!" he said. I eventually found my way home and got in around 4am. Claudia and Albert were still up, worried sick about what had happened to me.

Chapter 18

With the car, I was a young man on the move. Some of the major streets in the Valley today existed back then. Van Nuys was the westernmost street, with farms and orchards beyond; every weekend, teenagers would race their cars up and down Van Nuys boulevard. The only access to downtown was either the red electric tram, which had a stop in Universal City, or to drive east on Ventura Blvd. into Hollywood, then to Sunset Blvd. and Vermont, where there was short stretch of freeway to downtown.

I remember driving one day and passing a fruit stand that sold watermelons. I stopped and bought one to bring home to Claudia. Since the transaction was done through the car window, I just tossed the watermelon behind me, on the platform behind the seat. Shortly afterward, some traffic occurrence caused me to slam on the brakes. The watermelon went flying from the back of the car, was impaled on the stick shift, and exploded. Everything in the car, including me, was covered in watermelon, and I had juice and seeds streaming down my face. I remember a woman in the car next to me with a quizzical look on her face as she tried to figure out why I was covered in watermelon!

To find a job, I put an ad in the paper, which is how people looked for work at the time. I got several calls, most likely because of my experience working for the U.S. government. Within a few days of placing the ad, I got a job as a bookkeeper at Roscoe Hardware, in what is now Sun Valley. It was a straight shot down Lankershim Blvd. from Claudia's house to Roscoe Blvd. I was 22 years old and had only been in Los Angeles about 3 weeks. The delicious smell of the orange blossoms was in the air, the weather was warm, I had a car and a job, and I felt like the world was at my feet.

Still very interested in what was happening in the world, I would often go to a movie theater in Hollywood that showed an hour of news reels from around the world for a 50 cent entry fee. Upon leaving the theater one evening, I found a citation on my car. I didn't know what it was for and wondered how I could get a ticket if the car wasn't moving. The next day at work, I told my co-workers what had happened and showed them the ticket. They all laughed at how little time it had taken for me to get my first ticket, which was for having parked in front of a hydrant. The ticket was signed by Officer Chamberlain, and my boss, Mr. Forsch commented that he had a customer by that name. A few hours later, I was summoned to the front of the store from my office in the back. Officer Chamberlain, in civilian clothes, was in the store chatting with Mr. Forsch, who explained that I had just come to America and was not familiar with the parking laws. The officer was sympathetic and since he had not yet turned in his ticket stubs from the previous day, he found the stub for my ticket and tore it up.

In my spare time, I built a brick wall in the Karmazyns back yard. Our neighbor, Mr. Fahrer, offered his assistance when he observed that my wall was crooked. We were on friendly terms and he invited me to Lake Arrowhead where his daughter Audrey was singing in a play. Lake Arrowhead is in the mountains, about two hours from Los Angeles by car; I brought my camera and took many pictures of the beautiful scenery.

Upon our return to the Valley late that night, Mr. Fahrer told me that my share of the expenses for the day (gas, restaurant, ticket for the show) was $10.00. I was stunned and could not understand why I was being asked to pay when I had been invited, with no mention of splitting the costs. Not wanting to be rude by saying what I was thinking, I gave him the only money I had -- a $20 bill. He said he would give me $10 in change the following day.

As I was getting ready for bed, still confused about what had just happened, I remembered that I had left my camera in Mr. Fahrer's car. I walked back and retrieved it from the unlocked car. To my surprise, my neatly folded $20 bill was on the ground next to the car. I guess it had slipped from his pocket. The next day, Mr. Fahrer again said he would give me $10 back even though he had misplaced the bill I gave him. With that $20 safely back in my pocket, I told him to forget about the change!

With Allen Karmazyn in North Hollywood, 1948

PART THREE

MOROCCO 1949

Chapter 19

From 1948 to 1973, during both peacetime and periods of conflict, men were drafted to fill vacancies in the Armed Forces which could not be filled through voluntary means. All males aged 18 to 25 who lived in the U.S., both citizens and resident aliens, were obliged to register with the Selective Service. As required, I had registered upon my arrival to the U.S. and had signed a document indicating that I would report for duty if called.

In late 1948/early 1949, I received a letter from the Selective Service which said I had to submit to a medical examination to determine if I was fit for duty. When I received this notice I wasn't too concerned, assuming it was just a formality. I imagined they would do the physical, put my name into their records, and that would be the end of it. So I reported to an assembly in downtown Los Angeles for the medical exam, where I was deemed 1A (fit for service).

Shortly afterwards, I received a notice to report to Fort Ord in Monterey (near San Francisco). Now I began to get uneasy, for this was a time of tumultuous events in Korea. The Korean Peninsula had been ruled by Japan from 1910 until the end of World War II, when Japan was defeated. American administrators had divided the peninsula along the 38th parallel, with U.S. military forces advising the southern half, and Soviet military forces advising the northern half. Because of my passion for news and world events, I was well aware of the increasing tension between the communist government in the North and the capitalist government in the south. Every day on the radio, there was talk of Communism, as if it was going to take over the world the next day. Though the invasion by North Korean forces into South Korea did not occur until mid 1950, many young men were already being sent to that part of the world in 1949. So I went to Fort Ord with much trepidation, but seemingly little choice in the matter.

At Fort Ord, there were a series of classes to introduce the gathered group of young men to the army. During one of those classes, a sergeant asked all foreigners to raise their hand. Only two hands went up, one of which was mine. The sergeant reminded us of the document we had signed upon immigrating, indicating our willingness to serve if the country needed us. He then stated that since we were not born in the U.S. we would not be forced to serve, but that refusal meant we would never become U.S. citizens.

That's when my heart sank. Becoming a U.S. citizen was my singular focus and why I had left behind all that I knew and loved in Morocco. The few months I had been in America had only further intensified my desire. I knew unequivocally that my future had to be here, and never imagined that I could be denied my ultimate goal. Yet here I was faced with an impossible choice. I returned to Los Angeles with a heavy heart, having been given a few days to mull it over.

Claudia and Albert thought I was nuts for even considering going to Korea. "You've only been here a few months", they said. "Why get yourself killed for a country you barely know?" I thought of all the time, money and emotion expended to get to the U.S. I also thought of the many years I worked for the U.S. Army in Morocco, and the pride I would feel in wearing the uniform. I didn't want to renege on the document I had signed when I arrived in the United States and spent several sleepless nights, completely undecided about what to do.

I was looking for a way not to refuse and not to go, when something else came in the mail -- an invitation to Guy Dery's bar mitzvah in Rabat. That's when I came up with a plan. I would tell the army that I had an emergency in Morocco that necessitated my immediate return. I filled out some paperwork and got a six month deferment.

Chapter 20

Claudia had not seen the family for seven years and missed them terribly. Since I now planned to go to Morocco for the bar mitzvah, she decided to join me. I quit my job at the hardware store and sold the '35 Chevy for $100 more than I paid for it!. She packed up two year old Allen and the three of us travelled to Morocco in February 1949, planning to stay there for several months. Albert could not come with us because of his job with the Philharmonic. I can still see the tears in his eyes as we boarded the train to New York.

We spent a couple of nights in New York with Claudia's friends, then boarded the Queen Elizabeth I for the journey across the Atlantic. This huge ship, one of the most luxurious at that time, was beautifully appointed. Nevertheless, I was thankful that it was also one of the fastest ships of its day because the food was lousy.

After four days on the water, we arrived in Cherbourg, France in the middle of the night. We had to drop anchor off-shore because the harbor had been destroyed in the war and could not accommodate such a big ship. With my suitcase in one hand and Allen in the other, we descended a steep, narrow plank in the dark to a small boat which took us to shore.

From Cherbourg we took a train to Paris, where we stayed a few nights before boarding an Air France plane for a three hour flight to

Casablanca. Neither Claudia nor I had ever been on a plane before and it felt magical to be up in the clouds. The magic was interrupted however when I realized I'd lost my wallet. I looked everywhere around me but it was nowhere to be found. So, I stood up and announced to all the passengers that my wallet was missing. A short time later, I found the wallet under the seat, a place I had searched just moments before.

We arrived at the Place de Verdun apartment at dawn. Esther opened the door and she and Claudia fell into each other's arms. Esther and her husband Elie, and 1 year old Suzanne were still living with my parents, as were André and Maurice who were young bachelors. It was a joyous reunion for Claudia and for me, even though I had only been gone less than a year.

Chapter 21

Guy's bar mitzvah was a big event and we travelled from Casablanca to Rabat to attend. Claudia and Allen went by train with Renée, who had come from Rabat to see us when we arrived. In need of a car, I went to an auto shop where I had worked for a short time as an accountant and asked my old boss if he had one I could borrow for a few days. He lent me an old, war-era Jeep that had been modified with a wooden roof added over the roll bar, and two small passenger doors (most army jeeps had no doors).

André and Albert Assayag (the friend who had accompanied me to France when I first left Morocco) travelled with me. I took the wheel since I was the most experienced driver, Albert was in the passenger seat and André was in the back with his feet on the spare tire. Also in the back were lots of deli items that we were bringing from Casablanca to Rabat for the bar mitzvah.

Because the spare tire was not bolted down, it would bounce up every time we hit a bump in the road, sending André up with it. So I pulled over to let André move to the front, where he squeezed in between myself and Albert, straddling the stick shift.

The road from Casablanca to Rabat was just one lane in each direction, with open fields on either side. On this day, the road was wet from an earlier rain. About 20 km from Rabat, I slowed down to take a sharp turn, and the jeep flipped over three times before landing on its tires in a ditch on the other side of the road. The doors and back hatch opened and everything in the vehicle went flying out....except us.

Stunned, we got out of the car and stared at each other in disbelief. André and Albert were unscathed, with not even a scratch. My ankle was bleeding where I had been hit by the fire extinguisher that was mounted next to the clutch. This being a busy route, it's a miracle there were no other cars around at the time of the accident. I can only surmise that we survived because we had been tightly squeezed together in the front seat. The deli items, however, were not so lucky. There were salamis and cold cuts strewn about, as well as our luggage and the spare tire. Still a bit shaken from the accident, we gathered the tire, the luggage and what we could salvage of the food items, and pushed the car back onto the road. I wrapped my bleeding ankle with an undershirt, we squeezed back into the car, and continued on to Rabat. Many years later, I learned that Albert Assayag died in a car accident on the very same road.

André around 20 years old

The bar mitzvah was still a few days away when we arrived. Renée had a large house so we all stayed with her. What I had thought was a simple cut to my ankle became more and more painful. By the time I went to a doctor, the wound was infected. The doctor was completely inept and barely did anything before sending me home. Claudia was incensed, having spent the last seven years in the U.S. where doctors actually knew what they were doing.

I was in bed for several days and completely missed the bar mitzvah. Eventually, I went to see the same doctor again (there wasn't much choice back then). This time, he put stitches in because the wound was not closing up on its own. I continued to have pain and was still walking with difficulty several weeks after the accident. That's when I finally had an X-ray and discovered I had sustained a hairline fracture of the bone. The injury did not require a cast, but I limped for many months until it fully healed.

Chapter 22

Claudia, Allen and I stayed in Morocco for several months, during which time I rekindled my relationship with Juliette. I had been writing to her regularly and was overjoyed to see her again. Juliette worked in a pharmacy so I could only see her on her days off, or in the early evening before it got dark. At that time, dates were chaperoned so when we wanted to spend time alone, we would arrange to meet on the street, then go to the movies where we would hold hands in the dark. I later found out that she was not sneaking out after all; she would actually tell her mother she was going to the movies with me. Her mother was a modern woman and, knowing that I was from a good family, trusted me completely.

There was an innocence to our relationship, holding hands, stealing a kiss, but beneath that innocence, there was true love. Yet we could still not commit to each other. I was unemployed and just about broke, spending what was left of the money I had saved for years. I was not yet a U.S. citizen and therefore could not bring Juliette to America. And of course, there was my impending induction into the army. The thought of being in the army was made easier knowing that with my service, I could become a citizen in just two years instead of five.

Juliette and Yvonne, 1950's

Juliette and her mother, Rachel in Casablanca, 1951

Hardly anything had improved in Morocco in the time I'd been gone. There was a feeling of insecurity, and jobs and resources were still scarce. Many people were starting to leave for France or Canada. Poorer Jewish families with young children were being enticed to move to Israel with promises of prosperity. Israel was just one year old and needed young Jews to populate the new state. I realized how lucky I was to have an immigrant visa to the U.S. It was like having a million dollars in your pocket. Nobody else I knew could go the U.S. because they didn't have a family member there to sponsor them.

My siblings and friends were working very hard to make a living. Marie and her husband Maurice had moved to Agadir and Renée was in Rabat, but they would come see us at least once a month, as did Jacques and Solange.

Chapter 23

Once again, it was bittersweet to leave Morocco but this time, I had a different perspective. There was no longer any question about whether this was the right decision. It was very clear that there was no opportunity in Morocco and the only future for me was in the United States.

I was devastated to leave Juliette again and knew there was a tremendous risk that I would lose her. Now 24, she was a beautiful girl of marrying age and many other suitors had their eyes on her. Because of the circumstances, neither of us could commit to the other but I had no doubt that she was the one I wanted to marry. I was therefore more determined than ever to do whatever was necessary to get my citizenship and bring her to America as my wife.

The journey back to Los Angeles in July 1949 took us through Tangiers then to Gibraltar where we embarked on an Italian ship for the transatlantic crossing to New York. André accompanied us to Tangiers which, for someone who had never travelled far from Casablanca, was like going to heaven. Tangiers was a bustling, international city that did not suffer from a shortage of goods like Casablanca. I remember that André and I both purchased watches in Tangiers.

The ocean crossing took eight days to New York, then a few more days by train back to Los Angeles. Following is a translated letter written to Juliette a few days after my return.

North Hollywood, July 26th, 1949

Darling Juliette

After a very long trip (Tangiers, Gibraltar, eight days at sea on the Vulcania, New York, train to Chicago and LA), I am back where I started. Ever since my departure from Casablanca, I have moved from city to city like a zombie. My thoughts are continuously with you darling, and I have asked myself a thousand times WHY does it have to be this way? Why must we be separated again? At night on the deck of the ship with my eyes full of tears, I was thinking of all those unforgettable moments with you. I landed in New York without enthusiasm and have already started to count the days until we can be together. You are part of me and will always be in my heart. We are made for each other and nothing will change that. As we both know, the main reason for my return to the U.S. is to work for a brighter future for us. Also, if I serve the country after my deferment, I can achieve my dream of becoming a U.S. citizen much faster.

I know, sweetheart, how much strength you need to keep the other suitors at bay. Thank you for visiting my family. There was so much sadness when we left, everyone knowing it was going to be long time until we could see each other again.

Please write to me. I love you very much

Sidney

Little did I know that Juliette and I would be apart for another five long years.

PART FOUR

LOS ANGELES 1949 - 1954

Chapter 24

Back in Los Angeles, I had to start all over again as if I had just immigrated, except this time I had no money, having spent what remained of my savings in Morocco. After re-experiencing New York and Paris, and the social life in Morocco - parties, friends, lot of activities - the slow pace of the rural Valley seemed like purgatory. The weather was great but there were miles and miles of desert and farmland, and little else. It sometimes felt like I wasn't in America at all, but out in the middle of nowhere. I craved the hustle and bustle of city life. Fortunately, I would often accompany Albert to his concerts, which was wonderful. I got to see many famous classical performers of the time, including Vladimir Horowitz and Arthur Rubinstein. I already had a tremendous love of music and these concerts greatly expanded my musical horizons.

Though I didn't yet have a close group of friends and family like in Morocco, I was nonetheless enthralled with social interactions in the United States. Everyone was easy going, friendly and polite and it didn't matter who you were or where you were from. This was in such stark contrast to the French in Morocco, who were formal, reserved, judgmental and often times rude.

At the end of the six month deferment I presented myself to the army for another medical evaluation. I was still having some pain in my ankle and exaggerated my limp for dramatic effect. Another x-ray revealed that the fracture had not yet healed, so I was given another six month deferment. When I returned again for evaluation the medical examination deemed me 4F (not fit for service), and I was released from the Selective Service.

I was relieved of course, but could not have known then how close I'd come to almost certain death. By the end of the conflict in 1953, more than 36,000 Americans had died in the Korean war.

Upon returning to Los Angeles, my first priority was to get a job so I put an ad in the paper as I had done before. I also registered for night school at LA City College, taking classes in administration and contracting. I only attended school for a few months because it was far from the Valley with only a few roads to get there.

I got a job at Hollywood Ribbon Industries in Glendale. The CEO of the company, Daniel Des Foldes, was a middle aged man with a curling mustache who had made a fortune in South America in stocks and real estate. (One of his imports from South America was the song "Beer Barrel Polka" which became a hit in the U.S.) Mr. Des Foldes was born Jewish, but had converted to his wife's faith. His wife Eleanor was from a rich family and was not involved in the business.

Mr. Des Foldes was interested in my administrative background and brought me on as a temporary employee, replacing his regular assistant who had a serious illness and would be out for months. I agreed to a $50 a week starting salary, provided that my pay be reviewed after one month on the job.

The company manufactured high quality ribbon and had been a leader in the gift wrapping business since 1946. Strands of colored yarn from various spools would be collected in a machine and sent to several chemical baths where they were glued together, then sent to huge "ferris wheels" where the strands were heated. It was quite a sight to see these large wheels turning with a combination of bright colors. The finished product was then wound in special spooling equipment operated by female personnel, who were believed to have better finger dexterity than men. Mr. Des Foldes gave me a tour of the factory and invited me to make suggestions for changes and improvements.

One of my first changes was to contact the yarn and chemical suppliers to request price reductions on their products. After only one month, we were operating leaner, cleaner and cheaper. My salary rose to $75 a week and Mr. Des Foldes informed his former assistant that he would not be taking him back.

For the first time since I arrived in 1948, the American dream seemed to be within reach – I had a stable job at a company with many advancement opportunities, and a boss that liked me and whom I respected. I was able to put a down payment on a one year old Ford, which I purchased for $1,700. This car was the height of luxury compared to the old '35 Chevy I previously owned.

I worked at Hollywood Ribbon for about five years, during which time there were some major changes in my life. The first occurred about two years into the job. By that time, I was Mr. Des Foldes' right-hand man and was involved in many aspects of the business.

Mr. Des Foldes loved making money and the New York Stock Exchange was his passion. He awoke at 5am each morning to check on his investments. Being a heavy-set man, he was also obsessed with weight loss. When he heard of a quick weight loss program in Ensenada Mexico, he immediately signed up and spent 3 weeks at that clinic. Their weight loss "secret" was to put everyone on a very strict diet of grapes.... day and night... nothing but grapes.

Upon his return, Mr. Des Foldes bragged about how much weight he had lost by showing me the fewer notches needed on his belt. He had changed considerably in the 3 weeks and did not look well in my opinion. Yet he was thrilled with his thinner self and very pleased with the work I had done in his absence. He promised to once again review my salary.

A day or two later, I received a call at work from the Los Angeles Police Department. Mr. Des Foldes had hit a wall with his car and was critically injured. I rushed to the accident scene in time to see my boss on a stretcher, his face violet. The emergency responders said he'd had a heart attack just before hitting the wall. From that moment on, I pledged to never be obsessed with money or weight.

In those same early moments, it seemed that my American dream had also died in that accident. With the death of my friend and mentor, my job, my raise, my car payments, my whole future, all seemed to go up in smoke.

Eleanor Des Foldes was appointed Executrix of her late husband's estate. Being the only beneficiary of his will, she inherited a vast inventory of properties and stocks in addition to Hollywood Ribbon Industries. Eleanor knew nothing about the day-to-day operation of the business, but she knew that her husband had had great confidence in me. She had also gotten to know me over the years, and believed enough in my abilities to appoint me General Manager. She said her decision had been closely coordinated with the Los Angeles law firm she had hired to manage her assets.

Within a short time of Mr. Des Foldes sudden death, my job changed completely. I now had full control of the business including purchasing, sales and personnel. (We had a staff of 43, which would double around the Christmas holidays when the demand for gift-wrapping ribbon was high.) Along with a substantial increase in my salary, I was given an expense account and a company car (a brand new 1953 Bel Air Chevrolet), which enabled me to sell my personal car and save on the monthly payments.

There was no employment contract and I did not ask for one since there was a strong element of trust between Eleanor and I after her husband died. She had led a privileged life and was not equipped to deal with the matters thrust upon her after her husband's death. I became an advisor and trusted confidant regarding all aspects of her life, such as the poor relationship she had with her daughter, who had not been included in the will. She would call me every day, sometimes multiple times, seeking advice for her personal problems and I did my best to provide the counsel she sought.

Now that I was in charge I made some management changes, such as hiring new technicians with chemical backgrounds to improve ribbon quality. These changes resulted in increased sales, which greatly pleased my new boss. I relished my expanded role in the company and my future seemed very bright.

Along with my new responsibilities and higher pay, another perk available to me was a corporate apartment. Though Eleanor offered it to me, I declined since I really enjoyed living with the growing Karmazyn family.

In Hollywood at 25 years old, 1951

Claudia, age 31, in Los Angeles, 1950

With Albert and Claudia Karmazyn, 1952

Chapter 25

In October 1950 Claudia had a second son, Dennis. He was a sweet baby with a Karmazyn nose and Chriqui eyes. Baby Dennis slept in a crib in his parent's room. Well, I don't know if you could call it sleep because every night he would get on his elbows and knees and rock his crib non-stop. It was amazing that he could expend so much energy while he slept. This rocking was very noisy and kept his parents awake. I too had difficulty sleeping through the noise even though I was in a separate room. Claudia and Albert tried tying his crib to their bed, but the rocking was so intense that it would also move their bed! I had never seen this before or since with any baby.

At a very young age, Dennis knew that he would pursue music as a career, like his father. Dennis became a professional musician, playing the cello with the Hollywood Bowl Orchestra and as a studio musician. I think his childhood rocking was some kind of internal musical energy that he was born with.

Claudia worked as a seamstress in downtown Los Angeles and one of her co-workers had two Paris-born nephews who came to live with their aunt in the early 50's. Mark and Sammy Moreno were about my age and we became good friends. Also around that time, I took a weekend trip to Catalina Island where I met two French sisters on the beach, Mireille and Lisette. Their family had immigrated to Los Angeles from Paris when they were kids so both spoke fluent English. Upon learning that I was from Morocco, Mireille told me that her husband Francis Ravel was also a Jew from Casablanca. Mirelle's younger sister Lisette was 18 years old, blonde, blue eyed and very pretty. We became good friends and regularly went dancing together.

Whereas life in Los Angeles had seemed somewhat bleak when I first returned in '49, I now had a great job, plenty of money, a new car, nice clothes and an active social life. Mark, Sammy, Lisette and I would go dancing practically every weekend at the Ambassador Hotel or the Coconut Grove. Some of the American patrons were too self conscious to get out on the dance floor, but we would be the first ones on and the last ones off. I, for one, had been dancing since my teens and had a great love for music. This was the big band era so each night brought wonderful performances from the likes of Louis Armstrong, Frank Sinatra and Peggy Lee.

Another favorite hangout was the Cafe de Paris on Sunset Boulevard, which was a meeting place for Europeans, mostly from France. The Cafe was always bustling with activity and anyone with talent could get up and sing for the crowd. The ambience was great and the entertainment was free.

The food was also a welcome respite from the "health food only" at home. There was never so much as a cookie in the Karmazyn house so I enjoyed eating out when I could. Albert and I would often go to the Cafe together after he'd performed with the orchestra at the Hollywood Bowl -- needless to say I would not order dessert when I was with Albert! I loved Albert dearly, but have to admit that I would sneak "forbidden" sweets into the house when he was travelling, much to Claudia's delight.

Lisette and I dated for awhile, but our relationship was strictly platonic because I always had Juliette on my mind. I suppose Lisette eventually realized that our relationship had no future because, seemingly out of the blue, she married to a musician who was in the orchestra with Albert. I was shocked when it happened, but couldn't blame her for moving on. That marriage only lasted a year and she later married an older man who died in January 2013.

I lost track of the Moreno brothers until just recently. Mark was at LAX airport in the spring of 2013 awaiting a relative when he heard two women speaking French. He asked if they were from France, and they replied that they were from Morocco. "The only Moroccan I know is Sidney Chriqui" he said. Imagine the surprise when the two women, my sister Esther and her daughter Suzanne, told Mark they knew me very well. It turns out that Mark lives just blocks from me and has lived there for many years. I learned that Sammy died in car accident a few years ago.

In Los Angeles with my new car, 1952

Chapter 26

Though I was "living the dream", Morocco and Juliette were always in my thoughts. Telephones were still rare in Morocco so communication was only by mail. I wrote dozens of letters to Juliette, telling her everything about my life in America. Her responses were less regular, but with no marriage commitment from me it would have been improper for her to express much in her letters, which is probably why they were so infrequent.

With a great job and the money I had been able to save, I just needed one more thing before I could return to Casablanca and marry Juliette. A five year, continuous stay in the U.S. was required to be eligible for citizenship. The six months I had spent in Morocco in 1949 counted towards the five year time period because I had been on a deferment from the army. So, the clock had started ticking when I first arrived in 1948 and by 1953 I had what I so desperately wanted. I still remember standing in the judge's office as he asked if I was prepared to renounce all other allegiances. I could not have been more enthusiastic in my affirmative reply.

Here is a letter written to Juliette the day after I obtained my citizenship. Though I had previously professed my love, I was finally in a position to actually propose marriage.

Aug 6, 1953

Dear Juliette,

I now have another piece of news that will make you happy. Since yesterday, I am now an American citizen. I waited so long for this day that when it finally arrived, it seemed almost anti-climactic. I stood in front of a judge, with two witnesses, and after being asked some questions, was officially sworn in as an American. You, darling, are the first to know this. I am of course very happy, but will be even more so when we can celebrate together.

You asked in one of your previous letters if I am still thinking about you. What a question! Yes of course, even more so now that the time is near when I can finally see you after so many years. There is not a moment during these past years when I have not thought of you, and the great distance and passage of time have not diminished my feelings.

I often go out with friends and naturally, I have known several other women, but they were strictly friends. I never became serious with any of them because you are and always have been the only one for me. I have made no plans without you in mind.

I hope that your feelings for me are the same, since I am now thinking of a permanent union for us. As soon as I return to Casablanca early next year, I will speak to your parents about this.

I am proposing this now because I believe that I can make you happy, and I now have the means to support you with all the comforts you can dream of. I am even in a position to buy a house. The future for me here is very bright and I want you to share it with me.

I am counting the days until we can be together again.

Sidney

In March 1954 I went to Morocco with the intent of finally marrying Juliette and bringing her back to Los Angeles with me. Though it was supposed to be a four week trip, I did not return to live in the United States for thirteen years.

PART FIVE

MOROCCO 1954 - 1957

Chapter 27

In March 1954 I took a leave of absence from my job for a month. My boss Eleanor was very cooperative. Not only did she give me a small cash advance, she also paid for the airline ticket from Burbank to New York. I was to travel from New York to Casablanca by boat, which made it possible to bring several steamer trunks filled with gifts for my family. I sent the trunks by train 2 weeks in advance of flying to New York.

The Italian ship sailed from New York to Lisbon, Portugal, then to Casablanca. My entire family was at the port to greet me. In addition to those who lived in Casablanca, Renée and her family came from Rabat, and Jacques and his family came from Oujda. I remember Jacques and Maurice playfully arguing about who would be the next Chriqui to go to America. At the time, Maurice was 21 and single and Jacques was 33 with a family. I knew in my mind that Maurice would likely be the one I would sponsor, but I let them battle it out, not wanting to spoil the fun.

As the three or four cars caravanned back to the apartment at the Place de Verdun, I was struck by how small things seemed. The cars seemed small (American cars were twice as big!), the apartment seemed small, even the people seemed small. What wasn't small was the big buffet and large crowd at the house. All the neighbors had come to see me. I was a celebrity of sorts -- Sidney from America with his steamer trunks full of American goodies.

Shortly after my arrival to the apartment, I was in a back room when I was told that Juliette and Yvonne had come to visit. Under normal circumstances, it was not proper for a girl to visit a boy at home unless she had been invited. But after so many years, the two families knew each other well and, because of the occasion of my homecoming, there was no need for a formal invitation.

In the months leading up to my return to Casablanca, I had been thinking about Juliette and what would happen when we saw each other. So much time had passed and I didn't know if we would really get married or not. Perhaps she had changed, or perhaps I had. We had not committed to anything and it was very possible that our idea of each other was no longer the reality.

However, in the first moments when we saw each other, I knew we would get married. She was now 28, but looked 20. She was as beautiful as I remembered and I could not stop looking at her. All the years melted away when she looked at me, as if I had only been gone a few months. I could hardly believe that twelve years had passed since we first met.

I had intended to ask Juliette's father for permission to marry her, but she preferred that I follow the old custom of having family members request this on my behalf. So, my father, my brother David and Esther's husband Elie went to see the Gabays, where they were welcomed with open arms. My father knew Juliette's father very well, and they had both been anticipating this day for years.

With the formalities out of the way, I went to the U.S. Consulate to inquire about the requirements for obtaining a visa for Juliette. I was informed that, even once we were married, it could take two to three months for the visa. With only a one month leave of absence, this meant that I would be returning to the U.S. alone, with Juliette to follow later. Juliette did not like the prospect of travelling alone but there was nothing that could be done to speed up the process.

The next step was to arrange the wedding ceremony and the preparation of the *Ketouba* (marriage contract). At the time, there were three separate tribunals or courts for such matters. One for the French/Europeans, one for Muslims, and one for Jews. All Jewish Moroccans were married by a rabbi from the Rabbinical Tribunal. The rabbi also prepared the *Ketouba*.

I spoke with the Rabbi, who knew the Chriqui and Gabay families well. He was happy to hear of the impending wedding and would gladly write my *Ketouba* if he could, but he could not do so. "Why not?" I asked. "You are no longer Moroccan. You have changed your citizenship. We can only marry Moroccan Jews."

I was surprised and dismayed, not having anticipated this problem. He explained that the *Ketouba* included a provision for payment to the wife if abandoned by her husband. This provided financial protection since the majority of women did not work outside the home. The *Ketouba* was legally binding -- an abandoned woman could go to the Tribunal and get a judgment against her husband for the amount stated in the *Ketouba*. The Rabbinical Tribunal was granted the authority by the French government to approve and enforce these judgments. However, their jurisdiction was limited to Morocco. If I married and took my wife to the United States, the Rabbinal Tribunal could not enforce the *Ketouba*. He therefore suggested that I get married in the French court, which handled weddings for foreigners and which had a wider jurisdiction. With the marriage documents from the French, the Rabbi could then perform our religious ceremony and prepare the *Ketouba*.

So I went to the French court, known as the *Services Municipaux*, and explained my situation. The French court officer asked the following questions: "Were you born here? Were your parents born here? Was your fiancée born here? Were her parents born here?" When I answered yes to all, he said: "Then you are Moroccan. This court is only for French and Europeans, but not for native

Moroccans. We can't help you here. Go back to the Rabbinical Tribunal."

Now I was in a quandary. The Rabbinal Tribunal would not marry us. The *Services Municipaux* would not marry us. And certainly the Muslim court would not marry us. I could not marry Juliette in the United States because marriage documents were needed to obtain her visa. Furthermore, her family would not allow her to leave without first being married.

My time in Morocco was limited and I needed to figure this out quickly. So the next day I went to the American Consulate. I informed the clerk that mine was an urgent matter and that time was of the essence, which got me a private meeting with the Consul. I took my U.S. passport out, put it on Consul's desk and asked "Sir, please tell me what am I." He examined the passport and said "You're an American citizen". "OK", I said, "Please tell that to the French."

He asked who I had spoken with at the *Services Municipaux*, then picked up the phone and called him while I was still sitting there. The Consul spoke fluent French, and obviously knew the man on the other end. "Mr. Chriqui is an American citizen, not a Moroccan citizen," he said. "I would appreciate if you would perform a civil ceremony for him." They continued to speak for awhile then he paused and asked me "When do you want to get married?"

I had planned to have the religious ceremony on the 7th of April, so I told the Consul to schedule the civil ceremony for the 4th. "Go back and see the gentleman you saw before, and he will arrange things for you."

I returned to the *Services Municipaux*, where the French court officer was visibly irritated that I had gone over his head to the American Consul. The Americans wielded great influence and it was obvious that he wasn't happy about it. Long ago, the French had established separate systems for the Jews, the Muslims and the French, and he was very annoyed at having to make an exception for me. At that moment, I understood so clearly the power of being an American citizen. He told me to come back on April 4th with my parents, my fiancée, and her parents.

On April 4th, a group of relatives from the Chriqui and Gabay family came and we all crowded into the small court office. Never before had a Moroccan Jew been married in the French court. The court officer, with a sash of the French flag draped across his chest, was very displeased, and our parents were so proud.

Civil Ceremony, 1954

(L to R) Leon Gabay, Simha Chriqui, Renée Dery, Paul Harroch, Yvonne Gabay, Henri Gabay, me, Maurice Chriqui, Juliette, Esther Elbaz, Rachel Gabay, Judah Chriqui, Elie Elbaz, Bebert Elbaz (young boy)

Chapter 28

On April 6th, the night before the religious ceremony, the traditional *Henna* was held at the home of Juliette's cousin Fortune Moreno, who had a large apartment in the heart of Casablanca. Juliette looked like a queen in the *Grande Robe* that had belonged to her grandmother. There was Moroccan music, sweets and lots of joy. Unfortunately, I have no pictures of this event since the photographer didn't show up that evening.

I did not see Juliette again until the next day, as she was walking down the aisle with her father. She was stunning, with an elegance and humility that was rare in the American women I had known. Our wedding took place on rue Verlet Hanus at the Temple Beth El, which was packed with relatives and all the friends we'd grown up with. I wore a dark suit and a Stetson-made fedora that I had purchased in New York before boarding the liner to Morocco. I had seen the hat in the shop window and thought it would be nice to wear it at my wedding, if there was to be one. For some reason, I didn't want to wear a *kipa*. Perhaps I had seen pictures of some American celebrity wearing a hat at his wedding. Even though I was marrying a traditional woman, in a traditional ceremony in a traditional city, perhaps I wanted a little bit of America in the ceremony. Looking back at the wedding pictures now, I look a bit ridiculous with that fedora, though I certainly didn't think so at the time.

I remember marveling at how barely three weeks earlier I had been on a ship crossing the Atlantic with just an idea of a wedding, and here I was at the altar marrying the girl I'd had in my head and my heart since I was 16. Though we had spent very little time together since my last trip in 1949, I was certain that she was the one for me. I had dated several modern American women, who wore lots of make-up, smoked cigarettes and had many boyfriends. I knew I wanted a traditional woman as my wife and, in addition to be being beautiful, Juliette had all the qualities I was looking for.

I missed Claudia and Albert terribly and wished they could be there. They were the only family I had in the U.S. and we were very close. I loved living with them and they loved having me. Though I had many occasions to get my own place, including a company-owned apartment that Eleanor kept offering, I preferred to stay with the Karmazyns. I was also very attached to Claudia's young boys, Allen, Dennis and George.

Here's the infamous hat!

We had a traditional ceremony under the *chuppah*. When it came time to put the ring on her finger, I spoke the appropriate Hebrew words by heart, having been taught the passage by my mother in the days before the wedding. After the ceremony, my childhood friend Max Sebbag lent us his white Dodge convertible for a tour of the city at night, then onto the very elegant Hotel Noailles, which is still there today. Juliette owned a small car so the following day we drove to Marrakesh for our seven day honeymoon at the Hotel Mamounia. That hotel was the fanciest in the country (it still is), hosting presidents and heads of state. I wanted to impress Juliette by making reservations at the grandest hotel, but I too was impressed by the opulence.

With our flower girl Suzanne Elbaz, 1954

Wedding Invitation (left side)

Wedding Invitation (right side)

Wedding Day April 7th, 1954

*With my parents (left) and Juliette's parents (right), 1954
(picture of my sister Esther is on the wall behind me)*

My parents at my wedding, 1954

The first few days of the honeymoon were wonderful. We were so happy to be together at last. We talked about what our life would be like in Los Angeles, and how I would buy her a nice house and fancy clothes. My U.S. mail was being forwarded by Claudia so every day there were notes of congratulations from my American friends.

On the fourth day of the honeymoon, our happiness was crushed when I received a letter from Eleanor informing me that I no longer had a job.

The letter was polite and to the point. After some opening congratulatory remarks about my marriage, the letter went on to say that her lawyers had advised her to sell the factory. Though the company was doing relatively well, it was a seasonal business that only flourished at Christmastime. Because she had many other assets to manage, Hollywood Ribbon Industries was not profitable enough for her to keep. She suggested that I apply with the new buyers, who perhaps would be interested in hiring me. She also said that I had done a good job and she would gladly serve as a reference, but I was no longer needed and the advance she had given me before my trip was to be my severance.

Upon reading that letter, I was so shocked I could barely breathe. My shock turned to despair at the thought of being newly married and unemployed. I had made so many promises to Juliette and I didn't know how I was going to keep them. I was incensed that I could be so easily dismissed after all I had done for Eleanor. I was also furious at her timing, getting this news in the middle of my honeymoon.

Though I wanted to express that anger in my response, I thought it best not to burn bridges in case I ever needed Eleanor as a reference. So I wrote back a cordial letter that said I was very disappointed and felt that the small advance which was now my severance was poor compensation for the years of service I had provided. I added that I knew my worth and would not be without a job for long because "I could make a living on an iceberg". I never heard back from Eleanor and never saw her again.

Though I was confident in my abilities, I knew that getting another job like the one I had would be difficult. Temporary positions were abundant, but permanent ones were harder to find. I was thankful that I had saved a nice sum of money, which I had planned to use for furniture and as a down payment on a house, but which could now be used to tide us over until I found another job.

There was a dark cloud over us the rest of the honeymoon. Juliette kept telling me not to worry about it; she trusted that I would find something else. Maybe it was for the best, she said, since I could now stay until she got her visa and we could travel back together. In a way, she was happy about this development because she was very attached to her family and did not want to leave them. I too was happy to be back in Morocco, where I was enjoying the slower pace after the hard-working years in Los Angeles.

Chapter 29

Shortly after our return to Casablanca, I got a call from my brother Jacques (my parents now had a phone). Though he had come to Casablanca for my homecoming, he had not been able to get additional time off of work to attend the wedding. So he wanted me and my new bride to come visit him in Oujda, about 400 miles from Casablanca. He suggested that we could visit the tomb of the Rav of Tlemcen, a prominent rabbi who was buried in Tlemcen, Algeria, just a few miles from Oujda. This tomb was a holy site where people would go to pray and ask for miracles. Juliette's mother and her sister Yvonne were also invited so the four of us took a train to Oujda.

Within a few days of visiting the Rav of Tlemcen, I received a call from my brother Maurice. There was a job opening at the U.S. Base of Nouasseur where he worked and he had secured an interview for me. He urged me to return to Casablanca immediately.

After World War II, the Americans had left Morocco completely. But with the escalation of the cold war they returned in 1951, building three Air Force Bases (then called the Strategic Air Command or SAC) in Morocco as part of the network of Strategic Bomber bases. Their goal was to position B36 and B47 bombers throughout Europe and North Africa, within striking distance of the Soviet Union without the need to refuel.

The Nouasseur base was about 40 miles from Casablanca. The base consisted of airplane hangars, runways and a Temporary Construction Village (TCV) where the American personnel and their families lived. There were three entities at the base: the SAC that managed the planes; the Army Corps of Engineers, responsible for overseeing the building of the base; and a civilian contractor, Atlas Contractors, that was doing the actual building for the Corps.

Maurice worked for Atlas in security, stationed at the gate to the base, checking the credentials of those who came in and out. Being a talkative, outgoing man, he had gotten to know many of the base employees, including the chief of personnel for Atlas Contractors, with whom he often had lunch. In conversation with this man, Maurice found out the Corps was looking for someone who spoke English, French and Arabic, and had experience in contracting and administration. "My brother Sidney has all these qualifications", he said, "but he's an American citizen". "That's exactly what we're looking for" they said. The interview went very well and within days of losing one job, I had a new job with the U.S. Army Corps of Engineers. This was the beginning of a 36 year career with the Corps as a DAC (Dept. of Army, Civilian). It seems the Rav of Tlemsen really does work miracles!

I had about ten days free prior to starting the new job so Juliette and I went to visit my sister Marie and her husband Maurice, who were now living in Agadir. Marie had three young children, Lucienne, Roger and Henry. Just as my parents had given up their bedroom when family came to visit, Marie did the same for Juliette and I, especially given the fact that we were newlyweds. I remember opening the bedroom door one morning to find 2 year old Henry, standing on a chair, peering through the keyhole! To this day, I still jokingly call him a Peeping Tom.

Chapter 30

I worked for the Army Corps of Engineers in Morocco from 1954 until 1957 in the OAS (Office of Administrative Services). My job consisted of translating bid documents, evaluating equipment needs, and handling furniture and appliance purchases for the approximately 150 homes in the Temporary Construction Village. I was in charge of a large group of Arab workers who were outfitting the TCV. I was also in charge of a sizeable warehouse where we stocked various items. I started with a one year contract, subject to a background check. I was very glad I'd been cordial in my response to Eleanor since she was among the people they contacted.

This job was custom made for me. Having previously worked on an American base for four years, I was already familiar with base procedures. As a base employee, I had full access to the PX (store), hospital and commissary. I also was given a housing allowance which enabled me to move into a tenth floor apartment in the center of Casablanca; my father would often bring his friends over so they could enjoy the great view. Best of all, I was paid in American dollars. When I added up the salary and the extra perks like the housing allowance, I was actually making more than what I'd earned at Hollywood Ribbon Industries. Eleanor may have ruined my honeymoon, but her actions completely changed my life!

Because I only had a one year contract, I was hesitant to buy furniture or other household items, not knowing when I would be returning to the States. So we had only the bare necessities when Colette was born in March 1955.

Throughout Juliette's pregnancy, she saw a doctor on the American base where the care was top notch and free of charge. Juliette didn't speak a word of English so I would always accompany her to her appointments. After months of serving as her interpreter, I thought that perhaps she should start learning English, which she would need for our eventual return to the U.S. So one Saturday, I asked a friend of mine to come to our apartment to give Juliette an English lesson. That morning Juliette had not been feeling well but didn't want us to drive all the way to the base, which was 40 miles away. So she went to a local clinic where the doctor told her all was fine and sent her home. That afternoon during her English lesson, her water broke. She ended up giving birth at the local clinic, and that English lesson was the first and last she ever had!

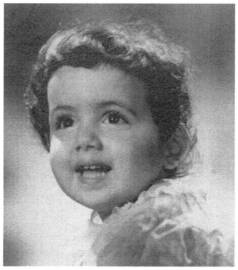

Colette, 1956

Shortly after Colette's birth, I went to the U.S. Consulate to register her as an American citizen. I was floored when I was told they could not register her as such. I had erroneously assumed that because I was American, she would be too. Had Colette been born on the U.S. base, she would automatically have been an American citizen. But because she was born in a Moroccan clinic, and had just one American parent who had not lived in the US for at least ten years, she was Moroccan. Had I known this beforehand, I would have been more insistent about driving Juliette to the base that Saturday! Thankfully, I later learned that because of my work with the U.S. Dept. of Defense, upon our eventual return to the U.S., my wife and children could be naturalized without the usual multi-year wait.

Chapter 31

There were regular flights between the base at Nouasseur and the American base in Frankfurt, Germany. As part of a morale boosting program, personnel could fly from one base to the other, free of charge, on their time off. So as a surprise to Juliette for her 30th birthday, I arranged for both of us to travel to Frankfurt in Oct 1955. Juliette had never been on a plane and had never left Morocco. The mode of transport was the C46, a twin engine prop plane with no seats, just benches on either side of the aircraft. The uncomfortable journey took seven hours each way, but it was free, so we really couldn't complain.

Having only lived in warm climates, we didn't even consider what the weather would be like in Frankfurt. So we were shocked when we stepped off the plane and were greeted by freezing temperatures. Since neither of us had any cold weather clothes, the first thing we did was go to the base PX (store) and purchase some essentials. Access to the PX, which was reserved for armed forces and civilian army personnel like me, was a wonderful benefit of working for the Americans -- we could buy whatever we needed, both here and at Nouasseur, at a fraction of the retail cost.

In Germany, 1955

We visited Frankfurt and from there, took a train to Munich to visit the Black Forest. It's unfortunate that I was not aware of the spa or "rest center" for GI's near Munich which I could have taken advantage of. Everywhere we went, Juliette would stop into the local post office -- which also served as communications center with a bank of phones for international calls -- so she could call home to check on Colette, whom she had left in Yvonne's care.

Chapter 32

The 50's were a time of great turmoil in Morocco. Moroccans were tiring of the French presence and there was increasing talk of independence, which was supported by the Moroccan leader Sultan Mohammed V. Believing they could quell the budding nationalism, the French deposed the Sultan in 1953 and exiled him and his family to Madagascar. In his place they installed Mohammed Ben Arafat, a mere figurehead who was not recognized by Moroccans as a legitimate leader.

The removal of the beloved Sultan resulted in an open and hostile rebellion against the French. By the time I arrived in 1954, there were riots in the street, boycotts of French products, and almost daily assassination attempts on French government officials. The French puppet, Mohammed Ben Arafat, feared for his life and was rarely out in public. Even though the Sultan was no longer in the country, the Arabs revered him so much they would say that his face could be seen in the nightly moon. Though daily life went on as usual, the streets were deserted at night, with people scurrying home as quickly as possible.

The Jews also loved the Sultan, who had treated them well during his reign and had saved them from being sent to European concentration camps during World War II. Yet, not wanting to side with the Arabs or the French, they were caught in the middle of the conflict between the two.

Though Arabs and Jews had coexisted peacefully for decades, it was an artificial peace created by virtue of the fact that both groups had been under the control of the French. Even though most of the Vichy French were anti-Semitic, there was great apprehension about what would happen if the French were forced out. With a fear of the unknown, many Jewish families began to leave Morocco, mostly to Israel or France. France was an obvious choice because of the language and the familiarity with all things French. Israel was just a few years old and needed Jews to populate the new country. Zionist agents were dispatched to Europe and North Africa to recruit Jewish families with grand promises of what life would be like in Israel. Though we didn't know it at the time, the Zionists also fomented some of the unrest to further bolster their case that it was no longer safe for Jews to stay in "hostile" countries.

To get to the Nouasseur base, I had to drive through several Arab neighborhoods. Sometimes there were roadblocks where Arab men with guns and long sticks would stop all cars to question the driver and examine the vehicle. I determined that the best way to avoid friction was to put a picture of Mohammed V on the windshield and speak only English. My car had USA plates, and I would show my American base badge and "attempt" to communicate in English and broken, pigeon French. I never let on that I understood Arabic or was anything other than an American. They would talk amongst themselves (and I would understand every word), then let me pass. Eventually, I became familiar to them and they would wave me through. Though the Arabs had no great love for the Americans, they tolerated their presence because the American bases employed large numbers of locals.

The Vichy French tried to control the Arab rebellion by many different means, none of which were successful. Eventually, France allowed Mohammed V to return in 1955, and the negotiations that led to Moroccan independence began the following year. Once back in power, the Sultan appointed a prominent Jewish doctor to his cabinet. Dr. Benzaquen is the same doctor who had cured me of typhoid years earlier. He had risen to great prominence since then, treating the elite including the Sultan's family. His appointment was meant as a conciliatory gesture to the Jews, however, the exodus of Jews from the country continued from that time forward. Morocco gained its political independence from France on March 2, 1956, and on April 7th of that same year, France officially relinquished its protectorate.

Chapter 33

In early 1956 when Colette was about ten months old, I was approached by a very wealthy man who was looking for someone to move into his apartment and take care of it for him. This man had an apartment in Paris and another in the south of France and wanted to leave Morocco for awhile until things calmed down. We did not know each other, but the Chriqui and Gabay families both had good reputations, and I had been recommended to him as someone who was trustworthy and honest.

His apartment was very big and exquisitely furnished - five bedrooms with French antiques, high-end furnishings, a grand piano, and the latest kitchen appliances. I told him that I didn't need all this room and there was no way I could afford the rent. But he was more interested in my character than in my ability to pay, hence he agreed to accept as rent the monthly housing allowance I was receiving. So Juliette, Colette and I left our sparse apartment and moved into his fully furnished apartment, where we lived until we left Morocco in 1957. In one fell swoop, we went from having just the bare essentials to living in the lap of luxury.

We loved having family over to our wonderful apartment and would alternate where we would spend Friday night dinner -- my mother's house, the Gabay's house, and our house. Both our mothers were elated to have us so close by.

Chapter 34

At the end of 1955, Marie and her family moved back to Casablanca from Agadir. She now had four children and the youngest, Corinne, was less than a year old. Maurice Ohana was very ill and getting progressively worse. One of his last outings was the wedding of André and Therese, which took place at the Place de Verdun apartment on January 1, 1956. By then, Maurice was so weak that he had to be carried up the five flights of stairs.

The medical care available at the time was mediocre at best and the doctors were not properly equipped to deal with such a serious illness. They performed several useless procedures and by the time they determined that it was stomach cancer, the disease had spread. It was so distressing to see Maurice in such pain. I wished that I could whisk him away to the American hospital at Nouasseur but I could not since he was neither a dependent nor a blood relative. I scoured newspapers and magazines to see if I could find anything to alleviate his suffering. I saw an ad for some pain medicine from Germany and ordered it by APO (American Post) to the base. This treatment caused his skin to turn yellow and though it seemed to help at first, the pain returned and intensified.

I would visit him as often as I could, telling him stories to try to make him laugh. I was in emotional turmoil -- I was very happy with Juliette and little Colette, and loved my job at the base. Yet it was heartbreaking to watch someone I cared for die a slow, painful death. I had spent so many years abroad and to now be reunited with Marie and Maurice under these terrible circumstances was very tough.

These were difficult days for all of us. We worried about Marie's future and agonized over Maurice's declining health. This was also a time of great unrest in the city, with the streets deserted at night. I remember regularly driving to Place de Verdun in the eerie silence of empty streets.

After months of suffering, Maurice died in March 1956 at the age of 34, just weeks after Morocco gained its independence from France. His death was very hard on Marie. She had four children and no means of income. Though Maurice had had a very good job in Agadir as the manager of a large theater, they had gone through their savings during the time of his illness. The family helped out where they could and we took Henry to live with us for a short time.

In the summer of 1957, Marie came to our apartment, despondent and in tears. About a week earlier she had given up custody of her eldest son Roger, then 9, to an Israeli Zionist group for them to raise him in Israel. Many families who didn't have the means to leave Morocco were sending their young boys with such groups in the hope that they would have a better life in Israel. Maurice Ohana's brother Max and some other Ohana relatives had already moved to Israel, and she had written to let them know that she was sending Roger.

Israel was still a very young country without much infrastructure and Max responded that perhaps now was not the time to send Roger, especially since he was so young. But Marie believed it was the best thing to do, since she was struggling with four children. She also thought that she might eventually join them in Israel. I was very angry at her when I first found out what she'd done. "I could have taken Roger to America", I said. But there was no getting through to Marie once her mind was made up. However with a week to think about it, she was having second thoughts.

Now she was at my door, sobbing and pleading with me to do something to get him back. Roger was at a camp about 60 miles from Casablanca and the group's departure to Israel was imminent. I immediately got in the car and drove to the camp, not knowing what I would do or say when I got there. I knew I had to be firm and could not take no for an answer. I was emboldened by the fact that I had a car with American license plates and had American Army credentials.

I somehow bluffed my way into the camp and declared that I had come to take Roger back with me. "But we have his mother's permission to take him to Israel. It's too late. You can't have him back", the camp director said. "His mother just lost her husband", I said. "I am now in charge of the family. She had no right to give him to you without first consulting me". This of course was a lie, but he didn't know that. "I will be taking Roger to the United States with me", I said.

At some point, Roger was brought to the front office and I remember pulling him by one arm, while the camp director was pulling him by the other. That's when I brought out the big guns. "I am an American and I work for the American army," I said. If you don't let me have him, there will be hell to pay and I will make a lot of trouble for you and your group." After considering this for a minute, the camp director let go of Roger's arm and I was able to whisk him away. When I returned home with Roger, Marie was ecstatic.

Chapter 35

When it came time to renew my contract, the Corps offered me the customary two year renewal. They were very pleased with my work and wanted me to stay. I also wanted to continue working for the Corps but only agreed to sign the contract on one condition -- I wanted the same privileges as Americans hired in the U.S. and sent to Morocco. At issue was "reemployment leave" and "household return", the only two privileges that I did not have. "Reemployment leave" was granted to Americans abroad every two years, enabling them to visit their families in the U.S. at the military's expense. "Household return" meant the military would pay to transport the family and household goods of service members back to the U.S. when their foreign service ended. Even though I was an American citizen, because I was already in Morocco when I was hired, I had signed a document foregoing these two privileges.

At the time I signed that document, I needed the job and didn't think about the consequences. Yet I had the forethought to tell them from day one that my family and primary residence was on Valleyheart Drive in Los Angeles, which would prove to be a very important detail. I now had a wife and a child, and an employer eager for me to stay. The contract renewal was therefore the perfect time to renegotiate the two missing privileges. I appealed to my superiors but they said I would need to get approval from the general.

General Lincoln, in charge of all the Moroccan bases, was stationed at Nouasseur and he and I were acquainted. Still, I couldn't just walk into this office so I wrote him a letter. The first part of the letter lauded the Army and the Corps: "I love my job, I love the Corps, and I'm so proud to be an American citizen working overseas for the Defense Department." Then it went on to say, "Even though I am an inhabitant of Morocco, my home and my family are in the U.S. It seems that the fact that all other Americans abroad have these privileges and I do not is a form of discrimination." The general agreed. From that point on, every contract renewal included reemployment leave and household return, which enabled my growing family to return to the U.S. every two years at the military's expense, and to eventually have them move my entire household back to Los Angeles years later.

Though I had written many letters to Juliette during the time we were apart, this letter to the general illustrated the power of letters for more than just personal use. From that point forward, I became a prolific letter writer, using them for everything from professional advancement to ensuring better customer service.

Chapter 36

I took advantage of my newly granted reemployment leave to bring Juliette and Colette to Los Angeles in the summer of 1956 with the intent of getting them naturalized as U.S. citizens. I knew we would eventually move to the U.S. and wanted them to have their papers for when that time came.

Because of my service with the government, I knew there was a policy in place that would allow them to get their papers with no waiting period. This policy was applicable to American citizens married to foreigners and stationed overseas, which was my exact situation. I wanted to take full advantage of this provision as soon as possible, in case the policy was changed in the future. Knowing that my time in Los Angeles would be limited, I secured a letter in advance from the Dept of Defense to the immigration judge, which stated that the naturalization of my family was to be expedited because my services were critical and I needed to return to work overseas. The judge reviewed this letter and gave Juliette ten days to study for the naturalization exam. We spent those ten days cramming at Claudia's house -- the three branches of the U.S. government, the provisions of the Constitution, etc.

The day of the exam, all they asked was "Who is the President, and where does he live?" Though Juliette spoke no English, she managed to answer these simple questions. That very same day, even though the certificate of naturalization was not yet prepared, I applied for a U.S. passport for Juliette. I still have that passport, with a picture of Juliette holding baby Colette in her arms.

Upon our return to Morocco, Juliette's father was flabbergasted that Juliette could leave with a Moroccan passport and return with an American one in less than one month.

Juliette's passport picture (with Colette), 1956

Chapter 37

Though Morocco was now independent, things in the country were still very unstable, and increasingly anti-Semitic. There was continued lawlessness and killings. Everyone I knew was worried about the future and it was clear with each passing day that we could not remain in Morocco. We had many family conferences in my beautiful apartment, gathering regularly to discuss what to do about the worsening situation and where to go when it came time to leave.

I was very close with my brothers David and André, who were still living in Casablanca. Jacques was in Oujda so I didn't see him often, and Maurice was now in the U.S. living with Claudia and Albert. Renée and her family were in Rabat, while Esther and Marie, and their respective families, were still in Morocco. My future was tied to the Army Corps of Engineers. My job and my American citizenship gave me options that my family and friends didn't have.

The granting of independence to Morocco in March 1956 and the French withdrawal created an uncomfortable situation for the East Atlantic District of the Corps. The agreement that gave the Corps legal status in Morocco had been signed with the French. This political anomaly, coupled with the changing focus of the division's work, led the Corps to decide to move its headquarters. The Americans were planning to build military bases in Europe and the Middle East, and were looking for a central hub to coordinate all this activity. Several sites were considered including Tripoli, Cairo, Beirut and Athens. Eventually, Livorno, Italy was selected as the best location. The Southern District was already there, so there was some structure in place. Most of the Corps personnel from Morocco and Tripoli were transferred to what became the Mediterranean Division in Livorno.

In 1957, with still one year to go on my employment contract, the Corps gave me the following choice: (1) I could stay in Morocco, but the job would end in the next three to four months, after which I'd be on my own (2) they could relocate me to the United States and find a job for me there or (3) I could move to Livorno and continue my employment with the Corps in Italy.

Option 1 was obviously out of the question. Everyone I knew was looking for ways to leave Morocco and without my job with the Americans I had no prospects in Casablanca. Option 2 was not of interest mainly because they could station me anywhere in the country and I was only interested in living in California. Also, I had gotten used to the perks of living overseas (higher pay, housing allowance, car, etc) and knew that all those extras would disappear when I moved back to the U.S. So really my only option was #3.

I had no idea where Livorno was and had to look it up on a map. I also had no idea what my job would be or where we would live.

The fact that neither Juliette or I spoke a word of Italian was also an issue, but I figured all the Americans would be in the same boat.

So in September 1957, Juliette, Colette and I left Morocco for Livorno. At the time of our move, Juliette was pregnant with Josiane. All military transport was still being done by C46 transport plane, with the benches instead of seats. There was no way I was going to subject my pregnant wife to this so I requested a commercial flight for us. When my request was denied, I wrote another letter to the General. We ended up flying Air France to Nice and took a train from there to Livorno.

We could not have imagined that we would live in Livorno for the next ten years.

PART SIX

LIVORNO 1957 - 1967

Chapter 38

In Livorno, we were initially housed at the Corallo Hotel, which had been requisitioned in its entirety by the Corps due to its central location and proximity to the train station. Though the U.S. Military had a base in the area, Camp Darby, the base housing was just for soldiers. So military officers, civilian personnel, and their families lived at the Corallo, pending the procurement of permanent quarters. Our offices were in the hotel as well. In addition to the Americans, there were many other nationalities at the Corallo including people from France, Greece, Libya and of course, Morocco.

I was the deputy to the Chief of OAS (Office of Administrative Services) and my work consisted of logistical support. Several bases in Europe and North Africa were consolidating operations in

Livorno, so my job was to receive furniture and equipment from these bases and assign them to the various branches. In the beginning I was in charge of ensuring that everyone had the space and equipment they needed, which was challenging in the small Corallo hotel. I was also in charge of coordinating travel of personnel to/from other countries. Later when I learned the language, I supervised a group of Italian employees and the printing of thousands of plans and specifications relating to multi-million dollar construction projects in several Mediterranean countries.

The first few weeks were very difficult. We had left an easy life in Casablanca near family and friends. Now we were in a completely different environment where we didn't speak the language and had to use a dictionary for the simplest of tasks, like ordering food in a restaurant.

Livorno was a small city, much of which had been destroyed in the war. During WWII, the port of Leghorn (Livorno) was the most demolished port in the Mediterranean. When the U.S. Fifth Army captured the port in 1944, they found it in ruins. Not only had the Germans destroyed the port but the Allied bombings during that time dropped more than 1,000 tons of bombs in the area. What remained was very old and cramped, like the Corallo Hotel where we were living and working.

Juliette had mixed feelings about whether we had made the right decision. She disliked living in the hotel where we didn't have any of our things, she was eight months pregnant and the doctor was miles from town, she missed her family terribly and she was frustrated by the language barrier.

Our friends the Sibony's had arrived in Italy a month prior and had nothing but negative things to say about life in Livorno, which further discouraged us. Yet, I knew this was a fantastic opportunity, being an American citizen living in Europe and getting paid in American dollars. The Italian lira was very weak, and the American dollar was very strong, which gave us tremendous purchasing power. So though I too had some initial doubts, I would tell Juliette every day "You'll see, this is a great place and we'll be happy here".

Our 1951 Ford was being shipped from Casablanca by boat and had not yet arrived so we had no transportation for awhile. In our second week, a colleague offered to take us for a drive outside the city. We were amazed and enthralled with the beauty of the Tuscan countryside, having had no idea of the spectacular scenery that surrounded us. We visited Pisa with its leaning tower, Torre Del Lago (home to Puccini, where he wrote his beautiful operas) as well as Viareggio, a vibrant seaside resort an hour from Livorno. The wide, seemingly endless beaches, the excellent cuisine, the exciting night life, and the annual carnival made Viareggio the ideal getaway. We were quite surprised by the elegance of the stores and hotels, and the wonderful architecture of the city. In the ensuing years, Viareggio became a favorite vacation destination, as did the beautiful city of Florence, just 60 miles from our home.

After getting settled into my new job, one of my first priorities was finding an apartment. Since the housing options in town were limited, most Americans lived outside the city in Tirrenia, twelve miles from Livorno. However we wanted to immerse ourselves in the Italian language and culture and wanted to live in the city. After two weeks of unsuccessful searching, a friend from work who had recently moved into a new apartment asked if I was interested in taking over the lease on his apartment. Though it was a nice apartment, he felt it was too big for just him and furthermore, it was too noisy.

I visited the apartment and found it was perfect for my family. It had a beautiful kitchen and was on the first floor of a new, modern building right in the center of town. We were thrilled and moved in as soon as we could rent some essential furniture, which was purchased with the housing allowance from the government. (We had little furniture of our own, since we had lived in a fully furnished apartment in Casablanca). The apartment was spacious and comfortable and once we got settled in, we started to enjoy the Italian life: the mercato (market), the outdoor cafes, the nice stores, etc. The American hospital was located between Livorno and Pisa at Calambrone just twenty minutes from our home and was equipped with the latest obstetric equipment, which greatly pleased Juliette.

Dino and Miranda Gianetti, the charming couple who managed our building on 110 Via Grande, became our good friends. They were anxious to please us and Dino found a maid named Inez to assist Juliette around the house. Once I received my car, I would often drive Inez home after work. She always asked me to stop the car one or two blocks from her house so she would not be seen riding with an *Americano*. She was a married woman and it was not proper for a *Livornesa* to be accompanied home by a male stranger.

Chapter 39

With Rosh Hashanah and Yom Kippur fast approaching, Henry Sibony and I visited the town's Jewish Congregation to inquire as to the availability of a Kosher butcher. I had a meeting with Rabbi Adolfo Toaff, whose son was the great Rabbi of Rome. When we told him that we were originally from Morocco and were now working in his city as Americans, his first question was, "Are your wives Jewish?". He was pleased when we answered affirmatively. As for the butcher, we were told there was only one in the city, Tito Rossi.

We visited his shop and while awaiting our turn Henry noticed a small picture on the wall -- the Madonna holding baby Jesus !!!!! He said to me "C'mon Sid, this is *not* a kosher butcher!" We went back to the Congregation and were told that, though Tito Rossi was not Jewish, he had been authorized to sell Kosher meat by the Congregation because there were no Jewish butchers. Furthermore, he only sold Kosher meat and no other. So Tito became our butcher for many years.

In the middle of the night on October 2, 1957 Juliette went into labor. Our building managers Dino and Miranda were kind enough to watch Colette while I rushed Juliette to the American hospital in Calambrone, where she gave birth to Josiane.

The next day was Yom Kippur, which I spent in a makeshift synagogue with a large garden. In the garden lay piles of broken marble, the remnants of a 400 year old Livorno synagogue that had been destroyed in the war. In that tiny synagogue I was quite surprised to see a U.S. Army Captain, the same officer who had helped Juliette deliver Josiane the day before. It turns out he too was Jewish and had come for the Kippur service.

Josiane, 1957

The following day I bought a beautiful red and white dress for Colette and took her to see her new sister. I was very happy to be the father of our second girl. Not only was she beautiful , but had she been a boy, the only person in the region who could perform a circumcision lived in Florence, sixty miles away.

When I brought Juliette and the baby home from the hospital, all our Italian neighbors were incredibly kind to us. There were no babies in the building so our girls were the darlings and would be invited to Dino and Miranda's house often. We had to pass their apartment on the way to ours and their door was always open. The girls, attracted by the wonderful cooking smells or just wanting to say hello, would just run into their apartment. Miranda didn't mind of course, but she did instruct the girls to ask *Permesso* before coming in.

Juliette's mother came from Morocco to help with the new baby. She flew from Casablanca to Nice, where I picked her up by car so she could avoid the long train ride between Nice and Livorno, a 150 mile journey during which the train made many stops. About a week after her arrival I was ordered by the Corps to return to Nouasseur on TDY (travel on duty). There were many army documents that had to be verified and completed on-site according to regulations.

I tried everything I could think of to avoid this trip, to no avail. Juliette was adamant that I not go, but orders are orders. So the next day I was on a train to Naples where a U.S. Navy plane was to take me to Port Lyautey, in the vicinity of Rabat, Morocco. It was a long, scary journey. The plane had engine trouble and we had to make an emergency landing on the island of Malta in the middle of the Mediterranean Sea. The repairs took a few hours, after which we flew to Port Lyautey, where a car and driver were waiting to drive me to Casablanca. Turns out I knew the Arab driver well, so I had him stop in Rabat where I surprised my sister Renée at her home. I also surprised the Gabays once I arrived in Casablanca.

I spent ten days in Casablanca with the Gabays and commuted daily to Nouasseur, where I was quite busy closing several pending actions regarding the District's move to Italy. It was strange to be by myself in Casablanca, while my wife and two daughters were so far away. I worked hard to complete the assignment and was so happy to return to Livorno. Though I had been away less than two weeks, it felt like I had been gone for a year.

Chapter 40

By the end of 1957, we had settled into our new life. We had two beautiful daughters, a modern apartment with wonderful neighbors, and I had a great job. Before leaving Morocco, I had visited a few travel agencies to get information on Livorno. They had raved about how beautiful Tuscany was, and they were right. Just twenty five minutes out of town were rolling green hills, unspoiled beaches and quaint towns. There was a local "American Beach" which was equipped with everything for GI's -- umbrellas, chairs, 25 cent hamburgers and 5 cent drinks -- we went there a lot! I would often go with Dino to the local soccer games on the back of his motorcycle.

For the most part, the Americans didn't interact with the locals, but we loved going to the *trattoria's* to improve our Italian. The Italians working for me spoke pigeon English or some French so we were able to communicate in the early days before I learned Italian.

Juliette learned most of her Italian from Inez, the maid. I took a few classes to speed up the process. Within about a year, we were both fluent and love the Italian language to this day.

That first *Natale* (Christmas) in Italy, we experienced how important the holiday was for the Gianettis, the building managers. They placed a beautifully decorated Christmas tree in the building's foyer and it was the center of attention for all the tenants. Since we were the only Jewish family in the building and we wanted to show respect for their holiday, I purchased several ornaments for their tree. It became a tradition that we followed for the next ten years - we would supply special ornaments for the Gianetti's tree and they would eat our Passover Matzos.

It was traditional for priests from local churches to visit each family in the building and recite catholic prayers while holding a large silver goblet with burning incense. When they came to my door, I would tell them that I was *Ebreo* (a Jew), to which they would usually answer "*Lo Stesso*" (it is the same). So it became an annual tradition that we would get blessed by the Italian priests at Christmastime.

A few days before Jan 1st, all U.S. army personnel and DAC's (Department of Army civilians) were advised to stay off the streets of Livorno on New Year's Eve and to keep their personal vehicles garaged. Shortly before midnight on December 31, we found out why.

It was an annual tradition for the people of Livorno and those in nearby Pisa, to do away with old items such as dishes, glasses, and other fragile items and replace them with new ones for the New Year. These items were thrown from apartment windows to the deserted streets below with a deafening noise, accompanied by the singing of opera. Imagine large numbers of breakable items flying out from the windows of every apartment building in town. You could not see the people, who stood in the middle of their living rooms as they tossed things out the window, all the while competing with their neighbors on who could make the most noise. It was quite a task for city workers to clean up the mess the next day, and all car traffic was stopped until the roads were clear. The first few days of January were busy shopping days for Livorno citizens, out to replace their discarded items.

Chapter 41

Livorno has a very rich Jewish history, which I was unaware of when we first arrived. The port of Leghorn (Livorno) was and still remains the main port of Tuscany in central Italy. In the middle of the 16th century its rulers, the Medici, decided to turn it into an important port and to invite foreigners to settle it. The official invitation was addressed to the merchants of every nation, but in reality the majority of its articles were directed to the "Marranos" of Spain and Portugal -- Jews who had converted, or been forced to convert, to Christianity (some of whom continued to observe Judaism in secret). The charter - usually called "Livornina" - guaranteed full religious liberty, amnesty for crimes previously committed, a large exemption from taxation, commercial freedom and the opportunity for Marranos to openly return to Judaism. Leghorn became an important center for trade, and commerce was transacted mainly by the foreign communities living in Leghorn, of which the "Jewish community soon became the largest and most influential. With the influx of Jews, Livorno became an important center of Hebrew printing and produced a significant number of Jewish scholars, intellectuals, artists and philanthropists.

The golden age of Jewish Livorno left many traces, including a magnificent synagogue built in 1597, with subsequent enlargement and embellishment that continued until 1789. The Leghorn synagogue was long considered one of the most splendid religious monuments of the European diaspora and was used as a model for the synagogue in Amsterdam, which still exists. Sadly the old synagogue was completely destroyed by Allied bombs in WWII. In fact when we arrived in Livorno in the fall of 1957, the remnants of the building lay in pieces -- beautiful Carrara marble in many colors, all tagged and ready for shipping to Israel.

The commercial importance of Livorno began to wane when Tuscany was annexed to the Kingdom of Italy in 1859, and other

Italian ports gained prominence. These events were reflected in the fluctuations of the Jewish population which by the end of the 19th century had diminished to 2,000 from a high of almost 5,000. By the beginning of the 20th century, the observance of Jewish religious practice diminished considerably, but the fidelity to the community remained steadfast far beyond the secularization process. At the end of WWII, about 1,000 Jews were living in Livorno; by 1965 that number had dropped to about 600 out of a total of 170,000 inhabitants.

In 1958 the construction of a new synagogue was started, funded in large part by the Italian government. The Italian government had offered money to the Jewish Congregation to build the new synagogue in Israel but they wanted it built in Livorno, on the same site as the old one, centrally located on a city square, *Piazza del Tempio* (Temple Square). The Jewish leaders selected a modern design in keeping with the original "tent of Jacob" which incorporated elements from the old building such as the beautiful stained glass windows. The new synagogue was already under construction when we arrived, and in 1962 I participated in the inauguration, which was attended by many dignitaries including the Chief Rabbi of Israel.

New Livorno Synagogue

Prior to the inauguration of the new synagogue, Jewish religious services were held in a small apartment in Livorno. Once a month, a Friday night service was held at the chapel at Camp Darby, which was located halfway between my apartment and Pisa. A young rabbi from Germany, who was also an officer in the Army, would come with a small suitcase containing a star of David, a few prayer books and a religious scroll. He would remove all the crosses in the chapel, put up the Star of David, then would hold a Friday night service for the Jewish soldiers and civilians at the Camp. I attended this monthly service whenever I could, and would often be called upon to read part of the prayers. At Passover, the rabbi would get large packages from the U.S. -- Matzo, kosher food, etc. I would always get one or two boxes, courtesy of the U.S. government.

Chapter 42

Living in Italy allowed us to travel easily to other European countries. In the winter of 1958, I piled the family into the car, along with Juliette's sister Yvonne and Yvonne's daughter Corinne, and we drove to Germany. The U.S. military had a rest center in Garmisch, Germany which could be used at no charge by military and civilian personnel and their families. Garmisch is a beautiful resort town in the mountains of Bavaria.

Since it was winter, there was snow on the ground and tire chains were needed to drive. Well, I hadn't properly prepared for this and my old tire chains broke. So the six of us (three adults and three young children) were stuck in the car in the middle of the Bavarian mountains on a cold winter day. I had no idea what to do.

After a short time, a car with several young German men came along. They pulled up behind us and got out of the car. I tried to communicate with them, but they did not speak English, and none of us spoke any German. To my surprise, and without saying a word, they got some tools out of their car, fixed my chains, secured them on my car's tires and drove off. We were astounded at their efficiency and their kindness.

In Garmisch, I was housed in the officer's quarters, so I had a wonderful room. I told them that Yvonne was our nanny, so she got a great room as well. One evening, we decided to go to an ice show and left the three girls with a German babysitter. We returned several hours later and found the babysitter in tears. Josiane had been crying since we left and the babysitter could not get her to stop. We knew that all she needed was her favorite pacifier, but we could not find it anywhere.

It was 1:00 am and I needed a pacifier. An Italian cook at the resort's restaurant told me where I could find a pharmacy in town. He said that if I knocked on the door, perhaps the owner would let me in. So though it was a freezing cold night, I set off in my car to find the pharmacy. Once there, I banged on the door until a light came on inside and a man came to the door. He had obviously been in bed and was wearing a nightgown and a very long hat with a pompom on the end -- just like what you'd see in a movie! Since I didn't speak German, I mimed as best I could through the glass door, sucking an imaginary pacifier and rocking an imaginary baby. Thankfully, he understood what I wanted and let me in.

Chapter 43

During the years that we lived in Italy, many relatives came to visit us. We delighted in showing them the beautiful country that was our home.

Maurice Chriqui

At the end of 1955, my brother Maurice received a visa to the U.S., thanks to the immigration paperwork I had filled out on his behalf. He already spoke English from his time working at the base in Nouasseur and wanted to go to the U.S. for better job opportunities. Maurice was a real go getter who talked to everyone and made friends easily. Though he had no trade, he was very gregarious and street smart. I told him he should go to school, but he wasn't interested in school.

He arrived in Los Angeles in February 1956 and lived with Claudia and Albert, as I had done before him. Claudia would later tell me that having Maurice in the house was very different from when I lived there. Maurice was rarely home, partying and living it up practically every night.

At the time of his arrival, the draft was still in force for all young men under the age of 25. So in 1957 he was drafted into the U.S. Army and sent to basic training in Ft. Lewis, Washington. He worked in the finance office, disbursing salaries to GI's.

Maurice in his army uniform, 1958

Soldiers were being sent to various U.S. theaters of operation and Maurice wanted to make sure he was sent to Europe. He knew everyone on the base, and knew everybody's business. So he made a deal with a Sergeant that had some back pay coming to him -- Maurice would expedite the disbursement of the back pay if the Sergeant could get him transferred to Europe.

There was a contingent of MP's (military police) leaving for Germany and the Sergeant arranged for Maurice to go with them. "But I'm not an MP", Maurice said. "That's OK. When you get there, just tell them a mistake was made and they'll find something else for you to do."

Maurice was sent to Pirmassen, a small town about two hours southwest of Frankfurt near the German/French border. After explaining the "mistake" Maurice was put back in finance, where he remained until the end of his service in 1959.

In April in 1958, I invited Maurice to Italy to spend Passover with my family. He obtained a leave of absence and took an overnight train to Livorno. The train station was very crowded, but we quickly found each other with our distinct Place de Verdun whistle (which we still use to this day). I had last seen Maurice in 1956 when I had traveled to the U.S. for Juliette's naturalization. Now he was a handsome 25 year old soldier who was extremely happy to see me and to hear the special Chriqui whistle at the station.

Once back at the apartment, we stopped in the building foyer so I could introduce Maurice to my friends, Dino and Miranda. While we were talking, with me as the translator, a highly decorated U.S. officer who also lived in the building came down the stairs into the foyer and greeted us. I proudly introduced my brother to the General who commanded the Corps of Engineers in the Mediterranean region. Maurice immediately stood at full attention and saluted the General. "At ease, soldier," the General said, then remained a few minutes to chat.

Maurice was very impressed and quietly said to me in French "I can't believe you know a general!" Then sensing an opportunity, he said, "Please ask him if he can transfer me from Germany to Camp Darby, near you." I did ask the General, who in turn asked Maurice what his specialty was."Finance," Maurice replied. The General suggested that he visit the Finance Officer at Camp Darby to see whether they had any openings. Maurice was in heaven at the thought of being transferred to Italy but unfortunately, the finance office had no need for his services.

Since Maurice was only in town for a few days, I wanted to take him to visit Florence. However it was pouring rain and very windy that day. When Maurice temporarily stepped out of the car, the wind sent his Military hat into the river. Without hesitation he got into the river to retrieve his hat. Now that he was soaking wet, we turned the car around and headed home.

He never did see Florence, but we had a great Passover at my house with the Sibony family in attendance, where we marveled at the irony and unpredictability of life. Here we all were in Italy, and Maurice was stationed in Germany, both axis powers during the war.

Passover Seder with Maurice and Sibony family, 1958

Lydia Chriqui

Around June 1958 my special niece Lydia Chriqui (daughter of my brother Jacques) took an overnight train from Paris where she was a student, to come visit us in Livorno. Lydia was and forever will be like a daughter to me because of the miracle that had occurred in 1945 when she was one of the first people in Morocco to be saved by Penicillin. She was now a lovely teenager, brilliant in her studies, generous and affectionate. Juliette and I were delighted to have her with us.

Anxious to give her the best vacation possible, we took her to several Italian cities including Venezia (Venice) and the island of Elba, just 20km off the Tuscan Coast by ferry. This tiny island (just

28km long and 19 km wide) had been occupied by various peoples over the centuries (Ligurian tribes, Etruscans, Greeks, North Africans, Spaniards etc) but none had done so much in so little time as France's military mastermind, Napoleon Bonaparte, who was exiled to Elba by the British in 1814. They gave him sovereignty over the island and allowed him to retain his title of emperor. Napoleon was on island for just 300 days but during that time, he carried out a series of economic and social reforms to improve the quality of life, partly to pass the time and partly out of a genuine concern for the well-being of the islanders.

His former residences, occupied by the Germans during World War II, had been turned into museums, which we were able to visit. The letter N for Napoleon was everywhere on the island and even now, over 200 years later, the *Elbani* (the people of Elba) have not forgotten him. Every year on the 5th of May, the anniversary of Napoleon's death, they celebrate "*una messa di Requiem in suo suffragio*" (a requiem mass for his repose). We were very happy of the discoveries we made on that tiny island and particularly how elated Lydia was of that experience.

Lydia did not stay with us long, but she left quite an impression on my family. To this day she is our Queen of Hearts and we love her so much. She returned to Italy several times in the following years with her parents and her siblings, Richard and Martine.

Claude Chriqui

In April 1959, we had the pleasure of having Claude Chriqui (son of my brother David) spend Passover with us. Claude travelled by overnight train from Paris, where he was a student. At 18 years old, he was handsome, intelligent and very witty. As with the other visitors, we took him on a tour of Tuscany during the day. In the evenings, we would stay home with the kids while Claude went out to explore Livorno at night.

Even though he didn't speak a word of Italian, it turns out he was quite successful at meeting beautiful Italian girls. He discovered that a group of boys and a group of girls would hang out on a central bridge in town, with the boys trying to impress the girls, and the girls acting coy. Claude joined the group of boys and impressed everyone by speaking French. Years later he told me how much fun he'd had and that he had very fond memories of that week in Livorno. We remained close to Claude and to this day, I consider him as the son I never had.

With Claude Chriqui in Florence, 1959

Claude and Colette in Pisa, 1959

Claudia & Albert Karmazyn

The Karmazyns, Claudia, Albert and their three young boys (Allan 11, Dennis 8 and George 5) came to visit us in August 1959. They first stopped in Paris, where Albert purchased a new car (Citroen DSi9) to take back to the U.S. From there they drove to Italy and spent a few days with us. I was so happy, having not seen them since I left Los Angeles in March 1954 for what was supposed to be a one month trip to Morocco. Now four years later, I was married, had two daughters and was living in Italy! They stayed in Livorno a few days and we took them to the usual cities and interesting sites around Livorno (by now, we were excellent tour guides!)

Together, we decided to travel by car to Morocco for Rosh Hashanah and Yom Kippur, and to attend my nephew William Dery's Bar Mitzvah. The 1,850 mile (3,000 km) drive from Italy to Morocco was done in two cars. The five Karmazyns in the new Citroen, and myself, Juliette, Colette 4, and Josiane almost 2, in my 1951 Ford.

It was a memorable trip along the Mediterranean Riviera De Fiori (Northern Coast of Italy) with all its magnificent sites such as Lericci, La Spezia, Genoa and Savona, then across the Cote D'Azur (French Riviera), through the Pyrennes in Spain to Madrid, then south to Algeciras where we embarked on a ferry across the Straits of Gibraltar into Tangiers, Morocco. From there we traveled to Rabat where my sister Renée and her husband Albert owned a beautiful villa.

We stayed at the villa for few days and attended William's Bar Mitzvah. It was quite a spectacular event, with an entire week of festivities. My parents and six siblings who still lived in Morocco (Renée, David, Esther, Jacques, Marie, André and their families) were in attendance, which made the occasion even more joyous since Claudia had not seen them in ten years. We headed to Casablanca a week later, where we celebrated Josiane's second birthday on October 2, 1959.

Chapter 44

My widowed sister Marie Ohana and her four children (Lucienne, Roger, Henry and Corinne) were living in an apartment in Casablanca. Marie was 36 years old and had been struggling financially since the death of her husband, Maurice. Despite the loss, Marie was full of courage and hope, and was determined to give her children a better life. In a bold move, and with great love and generosity, Claudia and Albert offered to take Marie and young Corinne, aged 4, back to the United States with them. The other three children would have to stay behind, and were taken in by family members.

Albert secured a visitor's visa for Marie and Corinne and when the time came to leave, the three adults and four children piled into the Citroen for the 200 mile (340 km) drive to Tangier, then a ferry across the Straits of Gibraltar, 965 miles (1,500 km) to Le Havre, the transatlantic journey to New York, then a 3,000 mile (4,800 km) cross-country drive to Los Angeles. Claudia and Albert's decision to take Marie and Corinne with them that day changed the future of the Ohana family.

Marie and Corinne lived with Claudia and Albert, as Maurice and I had previously done. Though Marie spoke no English, Claudia managed to get her a job as a seamstress. Marie's goal was to earn enough money to send for the three children she had left in Morocco.

Then something amazing happened. In the late 50's, there was a popular television show called Queen for a Day. Filmed in front of a studio audience, several women would tell a story of what they wanted and why. The audience would then select who they liked best and that woman was crowned "Queen for a Day" and her wish was granted. The wishes ranged from new appliances to dream vacations.

Claudia wrote a letter to the show about Marie and, just a few months after arriving in Los Angeles, Marie was on the show. Using Claudia as an interpreter, Marie told her story: her beloved husband had died of cancer and she had left three children behind in Morocco. Her wish was to be reunited with her kids and to bring them to America. Several other women also told their stories, then the audience voted............and selected another woman as "Queen for a Day".

Incredibly, even though Marie hadn't won, the show's producers found her story so compelling that they granted her wish anyway! They paid for her to travel to Casablanca to get Roger, Lucienne and Henry and bring them to Los Angeles.

Lucienne, Roger, Henry and Corinne Ohana with Colette on 5th floor balcony at Place de Verdun in Casablanca, 1950's

In October 1959, Marie returned to Casablanca to get her kids. Roger was living with my parents, Lucienne was with her father's parents, and Henry was with Ohana cousins in Agadir. Roger recalls having just a few days to gather his things, and no opportunity to say goodbye to his school friends. To them, it must have seemed like he just disappeared -- there one day, then gone forever.

The four of them landed in New York on October 23, 1959, which was Marie's birthday. Roger recalls being impressed that his mother was able to speak English and navigate the journey from New York to Los Angeles. Later when he learned the language, he realized that his mother's English at that time was actually really terrible! About two weeks after being on the show the first time, Marie and her four children returned to the set of "Queen for a Day" and were put on TV

Three months later in Feb 1960, a huge earthquake struck the city of Agadir. Over one-third of the population of the city was killed, including the Ohana cousins that Henry had been living with.

Chapter 45

We had a great desire to visit Israel, so in 1961 we arranged a trip. Colette was 6 years old and Josiane was 4. My mother-in-law Rachel Gabay, who was living in Casablanca, joined us in Livorno and was quite excited to accompany us to Israel. We traveled by train from Livorno to Venice, where we boarded a boat for the journey along the Adriatic coast to Haifa.

At that time, Moroccan citizens were not allowed by the Moroccan government to travel to Israel because that country had been boycotted by all Arab countries; Jews traveling outside Morocco were not authorized to return home if they had visited Israel. The Moroccan custom officers were carefully screening the exit and re-entry stamps on travelers' passports to enforce this policy.

I was determined to find a way for my mother- in-law to get on the ship without having her passport stamped by the Italians, or she would not have been allowed to return home to Morocco. Upon our arrival in Venice, I visited the Port authorities to explain the situation and asked that they waive the stamping requirement. Unfortunately, they explained, their operating procedures would not allow any such deviations. Time being of the essence, I contacted the Israeli company (ZIM) with whom we had booked our trip and asked for their help. I was told not to worry and that they would take care of it the next day at the embarkation point.

As promised, the ZIM representative was waiting for my mother-in-law at the pier and through some of his Italian friends, he easily got her on board. I discovered that the Italian custom officers understood the situation and worked closely with the Israelis. The ship was called *Le Phocée* and as I visited its various decks, they seemed very familiar to me. It turned out that it was previously called the *Koutoubia*. It was the same ship I had traveled on back in 1948 from Casablanca to Marseille!!

After a stop on the island of Cyprus, *Le Phocée* arrived in Haifa where a huge portrait of Theodor Herzl (the founder of Zionism) hung in the customs hall with a caption that read "If you will it, you can do it".

Israel was still a very young country without much in the way of infrastructure, and many basic items were missing. Meat in particular was hard to find and very expensive. Ordinary drinking glasses were not available; some ingenious Israelis found a way of cutting beer bottles to make drinking glasses. The impact of the Suez war with Egypt which had taken place in 1956 was still being felt, so the country was armed, with young men and women carrying machine guns in the streets. We visited several very interesting places and, of course, many of our relatives who had immigrated to Israel from Morocco in the 50's.

Jacques' brother-in-law, DéDé Barcessat, had recently immigrated to Israel and was very unhappy. Jacques had asked me to take some money to DéDé at the kibbutz where he was living. This kibbutz was in the middle of nowhere, with no paved road to get there. By the time I arrived, I had mud up to my knees. I was shown to his room and opened the door slightly, wanting to surprise him. He was laying on the sofa and when he saw me, he was completely shocked. He jumped up and hugged and kissed me effusively. I was pretty muddy so before leaving, I asked if I could take a shower. While in the shower, I was startled by a young female soldier in uniform. Not until that moment did I realize that the showers were communal, used by both women and men.

While in Jerusalem, I learned that an important sporting event was taking place in Ramat Gan, near Tel Aviv. It was the *Maccabiads*, where athletes from several countries were competing. Of special interest to me was the soccer game between the Italian champions (the *Juventus*) and the national team of Israel. I was very eager to attend the game but was told that all 50,000 seats in the stadium had been sold out for months.

Nevertheless, on the day of the game, I went to the Jerusalem Bus Station where a large crowd was waiting for the next bus to Ramat Gan. I positioned myself in the middle of the crowd with my Italian hat and a huge 8mm movie camera that I'd brought with me from Italy on my shoulder. When the bus arrived, people began to push and shove in a rush to board the bus. Being small and in the middle of the crowd, I was practically lifted off my feet and pushed inside the bus. I assumed the other passengers had combination tickets for the bus and the stadium entrance. I of course had no ticket, and no one asked me for one.

When we arrived at Ramat Gan, a large queue was waiting to get inside the stadium, all with previously purchased tickets. So I decided to try bluffing my way in. I asked an Israeli Official at the entrance to call his supervisor. I showed my U.S. Army credentials and explained, in English, that I was an American citizen working for the U.S. Army in Italy, and that I had come as a reporter to film the games. I had no ticket but had been told that I did not need one since I would be standing to film the action. After a discussion with another official, I was allowed to go inside to the press area. I think what impressed them the most was my movie camera, which had a big handle and looked very professional!

I was on the sidelines with a group of press photographers when suddenly there was a loud siren-like noise, and a group of motorcycles with their lights on escorted a black limousine into the stadium. The limousine stopped near where I was standing and to my big surprise, Prime Minister Ben Gurion got out of the car. I filmed him, as well as the soccer match.

I was extremely moved by the crowd of thousands singing the Israeli anthem *Ha Tikvah*. At half time, Israel was up 1-0, but I was confident the Italians would win and said so to an Israeli standing next to me. We bet $10 and he lost. After the game, I used the same technique to get on the bus back to Jerusalem. It was a day when I was happy to be small in stature!!

For the return to Italy, I once again was able to get my mother-in-law on the ship with no stamp on her passport. It was a memorable trip to a memorable country. I returned to Israel four more times in the ensuing years, more enchanted each time I went.

Chapter 46

While I was comfortably living my life in Livorno, my siblings still in Morocco were making plans to leave.

André had applied for papers to the U.S. back in 1955 when he and Therese were engaged, but by 1961 they still had not come through. So he decided to go to Montreal, believing it would be easier to immigrate to the U.S. from Canada. Therese's sister Rachel and her family had moved to Montreal five years prior so he knew they would not be alone there.

In January 1962, André, Therese and their 2 year old daughter Kathy left Morocco. The fact that Montreal was a French speaking city made the transition from Morocco relatively easy, though the harsh winters were quite a shock. It was difficult for André to leave because he was the last sibling still taking care of our parents.

For most of the first year, they did not put down roots, believing they would be leaving for California soon. But by the time their second daughter, Nicole, was born in November 1962, they had settled into their new life and abandoned any plans to leave. André remained in Montreal for sixteen years until circumstances caused him to again request papers for the U.S., which were granted this time.

With André in Montreal and Claudia in Los Angeles, the rest of the family in Morocco had a choice of where to go. David and his family chose Montreal. Esther and her family chose Los Angeles. Esther had sent her daughter Suzanne to Claudia's years earlier so she could be educated in the U.S. Claudia was delighted to have her, and treated her like the daughter she never had.

With my parents in Paris, 1963

My parents also eventually ended up in Los Angeles, moving there in 1963 after being sponsored by Claudia. Thanks to Claudia, Marie was also in Los Angeles with her children. Jacques' job took him and his family to Paris. Rene remained in Morocco for many years after everyone else had left, but she too eventually moved to Montreal.

Today I just have one niece, Renée's daughter Danielle, who still lives in Morocco, having never left. Her brother Guy also lives in Morocco, having returned after living many years in Montreal.

Chapter 47

Driving in Livorno, particularly with a large American vehicle, was not easy. Roads were narrow and aggressive drivers took many risks. One day in 1960 or 1961, I was driving my 1951 Ford in the middle of the city with Juliette and Colette in the car with me. I was on a main boulevard and had the right of way. Nevertheless, I slowed down at the intersection to check for traffic. The coast was clear so I proceeded to cross at about 30 mph. All of a sudden, a low, red, convertible travelling at high speed zoomed through the intersection, right in front of my car. I slammed on the brakes to avoid hitting the convertible. It was a miracle that there was no impact.

I pulled over and walked angrily toward the other driver, who had also stopped his car hard. He too got out of the car and walked towards me. He was a tall, handsome Italian and just as I was about to yell at him, he calmly said these three simple words:

SCUZI - BASTA - CHIUSO - meaning: Excuse me, enough, the case is closed.

My jaw dropped. With just three words, he had rendered me speechless. True, there was no impact. True, nothing happened to either of us, except anger that a very serious accident was missed by inches, and true, he was a very big guy!!

When I returned to my car and Juliette asked what had happened I told her that his three words took care of the problem. She laughed, knowing that I was never short of words and yet had found a faster talker.

It was quite funny and indicative of how the Italians are --- never wrong and using humor to diffuse difficult situations. It was an experience that I drew on many times during my career to illustrate how simple words can transform a situation.

Scusi, Basta, Chiuso became part of our repertoire and was invoked often in our household.

Chapter 48

In October 1962 the world held its breath as the United States and the Soviet Union stood on the brink of nuclear war. Throughout Europe, all American personnel, military and civilians as well as their dependents, were under great emotional stress. As the days passed the crisis increased to the point where high alert measures were put in place: Army dog tags (identification plates with name and blood type) were issued to all civilians including babies (Josiane was 5 years old, Colette was 7), evacuation orders were put in place calling for women and children to be evacuated first by air, while the men were to organize themselves for top alert duties, Defense Readiness Condition (DEFCON).

In my building on Via Grande, I was named building coordinator in charge of the evacuation process, which involved notifying civilian families when to leave and directing them to the military base for flights out of the country. This "job" did not please my wife. Like everyone else, she was very frightened and fretted that I may have to stay behind if women and children were evacuated.

For thirteen days we lived on edge, with the real possibility of nuclear war, heightened by the proximity of the Soviet Union and the belief that they intended to use nuclear missiles on Europe first. On Oct. 24, Russian ships carrying missiles to Cuba turned back, and when Khrushchev agreed on Oct. 28 to withdraw the missiles and dismantle the missile sites, the crisis ended as suddenly as it had begun.

On Nov 22, 1963 President Kennedy was assassinated in Dallas, TX. With this happening just a year after the Cuban missile crisis, there was grave concern that the assassination was somehow connected to the Soviets. No one knew if this was the beginning of an attack on the U.S. or if there would be repercussions in Europe. So as a precaution, all U.S. military bases were once again put on high alert, though things were somewhat less tense than they had been during the missile crisis.

The Americans in Italy were in shock, but so were the Italians. President Kennedy was a beloved figure and the Italians mourned his passing as much as the Americans did. All the neighbors in my building came by to give us their condolences, and it was as if a family member had died. A picture of President Kennedy hung at the entrance to Camp Darby and for several days, a steady procession of Italians came to offer their condolences. This outpouring of grief and support for our President made us proud to be Americans.

Chapter 49

Seven years after our second daughter was born, we welcomed our third daughter Sandi in May 1964. A few days before she was born, I had a vivid dream about my grandfather Abraham. In the dream, he said he was proud of me and the fact that I was an avid learner, as he had been. He was pleased to see that I was doing well, and I told him I was sorry I was not there when he died, but that I had followed his advice and had been travelling.

I hadn't thought about my grandfather in years, and had never dreamt about him before. So I was convinced that the dream was a sign. When I awoke the next day, I declared to Juliette that we were having a boy and we should start making arrangements for the circumcision.

A few days later, Juliette went into labor. I sat patiently in the waiting room, as all husbands did at that time. After a while the doctor came out with a long face, his hands in his pockets. "Are you Mr. Chriqui?", he asked. Then he put his arm around my shoulders and said "I need to talk to you".

My heart leapt into my throat. "Is everything OK? Is my wife OK? Is the baby OK?" "Yes, your wife and baby are fine, but your wife is crying", he said. "Why??" I asked. "Because you now have another daughter, but she is very beautiful. I wish she were mine because I have 3 boys", he said.

Though I had hoped for a son and was disappointed at first, I would not trade Sandi or any of my daughters for all the sons in the world. There is a Spanish proverb that says. "Lucky is the man who has a daughter as his first child." With three daughters, I have been very lucky indeed.

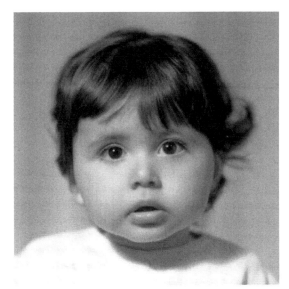

Sandi 1964

Colette, Juliette, and Josiane, 1959

Juliette in Rome, 1959

Juliette, Josiane and Colette, early 1960's

Livorno, 1960

In 1964, I was promoted to Administrative Officer with the Design Branch, responsible for management activities pertaining to projects located in Italy, Greece, Turkey, Pakistan, Afghanistan, and Saudi Arabia. As part of a committee of engineers and financial officers, I participated in the selection of a large US design and construction firm to perform multi-million dollar projects in Saudi Arabia between 1964 and 1967 (these were paid by the Saudi government). On the Administrative side, I was involved in developing scopes of work and evaluating the cost of designs as related to the construction funds available for each site.

To further my knowledge in these various tasks, I took many correspondence classes in such subjects as Statistical Data, Systems

Analysis, Personnel Management, etc. I understood early on that the more knowledge I had, the more valuable I became and the more promotions I would be eligible for. This was fine with me because I love to learn, so throughout my career with the Corps, I attended as many seminars and classes as I could, and delighted in receiving outstanding and superior evaluations.

Chapter 50

On November 4, 1966 the Arno river overflowed its banks and flooded the city of Florence, sixty miles from Livorno. At its peak, the water reached over 22 ft (6.7 meters) in some parts of the city. City officials and citizens were completely unprepared for the storm and the widespread devastation that it caused. Over 100 people died, 5,000 families were left homeless, and 6,000 stores were forced out of business. Approximately 600,000 tons of mud, rubble and sewage severely damaged or destroyed numerous collections of the written work and fine art for which Florence is famous.

Livorno did not flood, but for a short time it was surrounded by water and looked like an island. We watched the devastation in Florence on television and were astounded to see a shopkeeper we recognized on the news. Just a week prior, we had been in his jewelry store on the *Ponte Vecchio*, the famous bridge over the Arno river. Now his store and all his inventory were under water.

Soldiers and other personnel from Camp Darby and the Corps of Engineers were dispatched to Florence to help. Eventually, much of the world sent help to Florence to restore the irreplaceable works of art that had been damaged in the storm.

During the decade we lived in Italy, we would visit Los Angeles every two years, on Uncle Sam's dime. The Valley had grown quite a bit since my first stay in 1948. There were more roads and houses, and everything was modern and new. Though we loved Italy, we felt like nomads there. By now we had been married for twelve years and had three children. We wanted to set down some roots and buy a house in a place that would have more opportunity for our children.

The flooding in Florence was the last straw for Juliette. From that moment on, we knew that it was time to leave and go live in the U.S. So in early 1967 I sent my resume to the Corps of Engineers in Los Angeles and hoped they had a job for me.

In Livorno, 1960's

PART SEVEN

LOS ANGELES 1967 - PRESENT

Chapter 51

After the devastating flood in Florence, all we could think about was moving to sunny California. I wanted to be reassigned to the Corps of Engineers in Los Angeles where by now, several of my family members were living. However, it was not an easy task to be moved where you wanted, when you wanted, to the job you wanted. If you wished to move back to the States, you had to accept what was available, regardless of where it was in the country. Nevertheless in early 1967, I sent a detailed resume of my experience to the Military side of the Corps in Los Angeles and hoped they had an opening for me. I knew they were involved with some large construction projects for which I believed my experience would be perfectly suited.

It did not take long for my resume to land right where it needed to be. In February 1967 I received a letter from Mr. Olson, the Chief of the Military Planning Branch of the Los Angeles Engineering Division. The letter said in part: "My Branch is responsible for project management of all the Army, Air Force and NASA programs assigned to the Los Angeles District. Reading the duties of your present position in Italy indicates that the position I have open is the same thing you are doing now and I am definitely interested in getting you here as soon as possible. You can expect to receive an official request for your release and transfer within the next few weeks."

Wow! I was amazed at the speed with which I received a response, and the timing could not have been better. Juliette was anxious to leave Italy and finally live in the U.S. Though I agreed that it was time to go, I had mixed feelings about leaving Europe. We had a very good life in Italy. Two of my daughters were born there and we were constantly travelling and visiting interesting places. My job entitled me to many privileges that I would lose in relocating to the U.S. including my substantial housing allowance and access to the PX and commissary where we could buy things, including gas, at a fraction of their retail value. After thirteen years of government service in Morocco and Europe this would be a huge change for me and my family. On the other hand, I knew it was time for us to be in a permanent home near relatives and to offer my daughters a future in the United States.

When the call came from Los Angeles asking when I was available to start, my office in Italy was flabbergasted. Until then, they had no idea that I wanted to leave. "Are you sure you want to go?" they asked. "You have it good here. Everything is paid for. Many people who have left are begging to come back."

But I had always planned on living in the U.S. and after a ten year "detour" to Italy, it was time. Colette was almost 12 and Josiane was 9 -- if I stayed any longer it would have been very difficult for them to transition to life in the U.S. as teenagers. Thankfully, they spoke fluent English because they had attended the American school on the base. Sandi was only 2, so there were no language or culture issues for her.

For our trip back to the US, we were scheduled to fly to Los Angeles, but I wanted one last Mediterranean experience and a final transatlantic journey since I would probably never again have that opportunity.

The American Constitution was THE luxury ocean liner at that time and we spent eight wonderful days on that ship, first enjoying a Mediterranean cruise, then across the Atlantic to New York.

Leaving Italy - On Cruise to New York, 1967

While on the ship, we met a Moroccan purser name Lillo Suissa. He was so excited to have fellow Moroccans on board that he set us up in a first class cabin. We sailed in March 1967, which I remember clearly because we celebrated Colette's 12th birthday on the ship and the orchestra played Happy Birthday for her.

Chapter 52

When we arrived in Los Angeles, the family was ecstatic, as were we. By now, three of my siblings, Claudia, Marie, Maurice and their families, were living in the Valley, in close proximity to each other. My parents were also here, having left Morocco in 1963.

I had saved enough money to put a down payment on a house and buy a car. We started looking for a house right away, while living temporarily in a furnished three bedroom apartment on Burbank Blvd. just down the street from my parent's apartment. We were authorized to have our housing expenses paid by the Corps for three months until we could get settled and receive our household items. However, the three months ended and we hadn't yet found a house that we liked and could afford. So I pulled some strings to get our housing allowance extended for another three months and had our furniture put into storage upon its arrival.

I did buy a car right away -- a Pontiac LeSabre. It was my first new car in about 15 years and wow, was it nice! So nice in fact that Claudia bought the same one, as did my nephew Gabriel Dery (son of Renée).

After six months of searching, we bought a house in Sept 1967 for $41,000, which was an average price for a house at that time. I could never have imagined that 46 years later, I would still be living in that house! Our decision to buy the house on Aetna Street in Van Nuys was influenced by several factors -- the modern appliances, the proximity and reputation of the nearby schools, and the fact that my parents and siblings all lived within five miles.

After so many years away from my family, it was such a joy to have some of them close by. (By this time, Jacques had settled in Paris, David and André were in Montreal, and only Renée remained in Morocco.) Many family friends had also moved to Los Angeles and my parents' apartment became the "Casino", where there was always a game of cards being played. They loved the life here, surrounded by family and friends. Everyone -- siblings, nieces, nephews, friends - would gather at their house every Saturday for *Dafina*.

Though this was great for me, it was a constant reminder to Juliette of how far she was from her family in Morocco and how much she missed them. So within a few months of arriving, I started working on bringing her parents and siblings to Los Angeles.

Chapter 53

For months prior to leaving Italy, Juliette and I talked about going to America. We and the girls were excited and filled with anticipation of what was to come. However once here, it didn't take long for the excitement to wear off and for reality to set in. It was a very hard adjustment for all of us, except Sandi because she was so young.

For Juliette, Van Nuys *was* America. There was abundance everywhere with big supermarkets and shopping malls. She had all the modern conveniences and appliances, only some of which we'd had in Livorno, but none of which had been ours (all our household items had been rented). She had the great weather, which was a major factor in deciding to leave Italy, for she would rue the cold and rain of the winter months in Livorno after returning from our annual trips to California.

However, whereas in Italy she had been treated like a queen, here she was isolated in her big house with none of her family and no friends. Her sister Yvonne had lived with us for six months in Italy before moving to Canada and Juliette missed her terribly. In Italy, just about everything had been paid for or was available to us at the Base PX for a ridiculously low price. We were not used to paying out of pocket for everyday necessities and we were shocked at the prices.

To afford the luxury that we had in Italy, Juliette would have had to work, but I wanted her to stay home to raise the kids. Having lived with the Karmazyns, I had seen firsthand what is was like for the kids to have both parents working. Albert travelled a lot and was not close with his boys, who were on their own after school because Claudia was at work. I didn't want that for my girls.

Even if I hadn't felt so strongly about Juliette being a stay-at-home mom, it was unlikely that she could have found a job because she did not drive and did not speak English. Whereas Italian had come to her relatively easily, the same could not be said for English, and she struggled with the language. Though she'd had a driver's license in Italy, the language barrier made it impossible for her to pass the written portion of the California driving test. She eventually took some night classes in English and passed the driving test, with some surreptitious help from me. She even volunteered in a hospital for a short time but she never mastered English, which was a source of endless frustration for her.

Colette and Josiane were fluent in English so the language was not an issue for them. Still, they were miserable here. All the talk about coming to America had made them expect Disneyland every day so the reality of life here was a rude awakening.

They entered school in the middle of the term (March 1967), which is always difficult. Not only were they the new kids, they were the new kids from another country. The teachers loved them because they were very polite and well behaved, but the school kids thought they were odd. They didn't dress like the other kids, they didn't act like them and they didn't talk like them.

In Italy during the warmer months, the girls and Juliette spent practically every day after school, and most of the summer, at the beach just a few miles out of town. In fact, the girls have memories of doing their homework at the beach. I would join them every day after 2:30pm since I was working on flex time, going into work early so I could leave early. Though Los Angeles has beaches and nicer weather than Livorno for a good part of the year, it was impossible to go to the beach after school since it was much further away and we only had one car, which I would take to work.

I too was a bit lost in Los Angeles. I had to drive downtown for work, and I wasn't used to the freeways and the heavy traffic. I also wasn't used to the regiment of staying in one lane because Italian roads had no lanes. Until I got acclimated to driving here, every day I felt like my life was in the hands of the guy next to me on the freeway -- what if he didn't stay in his lane?

I missed living in Europe. I missed how you could drive a few hours and be in a different country. I missed the great museums, the art, the operas, the architecture, none of which we had in the Valley. Livorno was a small town, but we had lived in the center where there was always activity. Every morning, the shopkeepers would sing as they swept their sidewalks. I knew all my neighbors and loved the social interaction. I missed the pace of Italian life, which was much slower than here. In Los Angeles, I was working hard, dealing with the freeways, had no social life (other than family) and few opportunities for travel.

There were many times when I felt I it was a mistake to have left Italy and to this day, I've never become fully Americanized. We were all frustrated and on edge, except for Sandi who was too young to notice the difference between Livorno and Los Angeles. Juliette and I argued a lot in the first few years here, something we had never done before. We were all under stress at the dramatic change in our lives, stress which manifested itself in high blood pressure for me and a breast cyst for Juliette. Thankfully, it was not cancerous, but the health scare only added to the pressure we were all under.

Though Colette and Josiane eventually made friends, they never felt comfortable in the hustle and bustle of Los Angeles and at their first opportunity, they both moved to Northern California, where they still live today. Colette went to Santa Cruz, a small beach town on the coast, and Josiane moved to San Francisco, known as the City by the Bay. I guess they have the beach in their blood.

Chapter 54

I reported to Federal Building in Downtown Los Angeles and was amazed to discover that the division I would be working for occupied the entire 6th floor and had almost 1,400 employees. In Italy, the staff was relatively small and everyone knew who I was. Here I was a small fish in a very big pond.

My initial job was as Military Planning Manager of Bases. My division was in charge of all Air Force bases in California and Nevada, as well as some NASA projects and some "defense of coastline" projects. There was plenty of work and I dove right in. I was in that position just one year, during which time I changed a lot of procedures and became well known in my department.

One day my boss said to me, "Much as I'd like to keep you, there is an opening in Administrative Services for a job that is right up your alley. It's a higher pay grade and you'll be working directly under the District Engineer, Colonel Norman Pherson, who is in command of the L.A. Corps of Engineers Office."

I was now in charge of sixty two employees, most of whom didn't know what to make of me -- this short, Jewish foreigner with an accent. There was some resentment at first -- who was I and why had I been put in charge?

In Italy I had supervised a much smaller group however I had worked for a Division office whereas this was only a District office. Therefore I felt confident that I could do the job and welcomed the opportunity. My years of experience had also taught me how to handle all kinds of people by treating everyone with respect and an open mind, while remaining firm about my expectations.

I remember one woman with thiry years of service who was upset because I had taken her parking space. My predecessor didn't drive so he had given her his assigned parking space. She said "if you take my space, I will resign" to which I answered "I'll be sorry to lose you". She complained to the Colonel, but I kept my parking space and she didn't resign.

Chapter 55

A few months after we arrived in Los Angeles, the Six-Day War was fought in the Middle East in June 1967. The Israelis defended the war as a preventative military effort to counter what they saw as an impending attack by the Arab nations that surrounded Israel. The Israelis launched a hugely successful military campaign against its perceived enemies. The air forces of Egypt, Jordan, Syria and Iraq were all but destroyed on June 5th. By June 7th, many Egyptian tanks had been destroyed in the Sinai Desert and Israeli forces had reached the Suez Canal. On the same day, the entire west bank of the Jordan River was cleared of Jordanian forces. The Golan Heights were captured from Syria and Israeli forces moved 30 miles into Syria itself.

The war was a military disaster for the Arabs and dealt a massive blow to the Arabs' morale, leading to increased Arab-Jewish tensions worldwide including in Morocco. Moroccan Jews feared retaliation by Arabs and thus began another wave of departures. In reality, there was little or no retaliation in Morocco but nevertheless, the exodus of Jews continued. By 1971 the Jewish population had dwindled to 35,000 from 265,000 in 1948. Only about 2,500 Jews live there now.

In light of these world events, Juliette's parents were very anxious to leave Morocco, and we were eager to have them join us in Los Angeles. Since Juliette was a U.S. citizen, she sponsored her parents to come to America, and once here, they in turn sponsored their children Yvonne and Henri to come as well. I did all the paperwork of course, which I was happy to do since I loved Juliette's family. The Gabay's were like second parents to me. They never called me Sidney -- they called me "mon fils" (my son).

I got Juliette's parents an apartment around the corner from our house. At first, they were very happy to be out of Morocco and living so close to us. But they too had tremendous difficulty adjusting to their new lives. Leon Gabay had been a bank director in Casablanca and was well known and well respected in the community. In Los Angeles, he didn't work, didn't speak English and had few friends. Every time we would drive by a bank, he would marvel at how many banks we had, and there would be a wistful look in his eyes.

Leon had a heart condition whereby his heart would beat very fast. I would press on a vein in his neck to regulate the heartbeat. The longing for home and regret about the move further exacerbated his heart condition.

Nostalgia can sometimes blind someone to the realities of what they left behind, and when he took a trip to Morocco in the early 70's he realized that all was not as rosy as he remembered. Still, the nostalgia and regret never left him and he died in 1975. He was a sweet, elegant man and his passing was very hard on all of us. Yes, he had a medical condition but we believe he died of a broken heart.

Rachel and Leon Gabay in Casablanca, early 1970's

After Leon's passing, Juliette's mother became very ill, ending up in a home for seven long years. Juliette and Yvonne visited her three times a day, which took quite a toll on them. Until the end, their mother was lucid and alert. Despite her long illness, she never complained, always saying that "this is what *Hashem* wants".

Juliette and her sister Yvonne were very close, like twins. After Juliette got married, Yvonne also married shortly thereafter. That marriage didn't last a year, but it did produce a daughter, Corinne. While we were living in Italy, Yvonne and Corinne would often come to visit for weeks or months at a time. In our last years in Italy, Yvonne started immigration proceedings to Canada. She wanted to go to the U.S. but it was impossible to get immigration papers without a family sponsor. We knew we would eventually settle in the U.S., at which time Juliette could file the necessary papers to have Yvonne join us.

Wanting to leave Morocco, and knowing it would be easier to immigrate to the U.S. from Canada, Yvonne moved to Montreal in the early 60's. Once Juliette's parents were in Los Angeles, they sponsored Yvonne to come join them here. Juliette was overjoyed to have her "twin" close by once more. They became as inseparable as they had been in their youth, and Yvonne was just as devastated as I was when Juliette died.

Juliette's brother, Henri was an adventurer and a rebel who was very intelligent and spoke many languages. During WWII Henri was, of course, a Moroccan citizen. But all his friends were French citizens. So, when a truck took all his friends to fight for France, he climbed in and went with them. He changed his name, said he was French, and went to war in France and Germany even though he was under no obligation to do so.

Henri Gabay in French army uniform, 1940's

Henri was living in Israel in the early 70's when his mother, now in Los Angeles, sponsored him to come to America. Henri lived in Los Angeles for a short time, working as a wine broker, but eventually moved to San Francisco where he married a non-Jewish woman, much to his family's chagrin.

Henri was a heavy smoker and got adult-onset diabetes in his later years. His diabetes was not well managed and he had one leg amputated. Eventually, the disease progressed and the other leg needed to be amputated, at which point he didn't want to live anymore. One night, he pulled all the wires out and died in 1999 at the age of 76.

A few days before he passed away, he called me. I made him promise not to be cremated, which is what his wife wanted. In the Jewish religion, your body needs to be whole when it is buried, so cremation is not permitted. His wife cremated him anyway and we cut all ties with her.

In 1968, my sister Esther and her husband Elie Elbaz moved to Los Angeles from Morocco. The following year, Elie became very ill. I have always been very concerned and willing to help in any way possible when a member of the family is ill. Since the hospital was near where I worked, I would visit him every day during my lunch hour.

When he died, I took care of his funeral arrangements with my brother Maurice, and I prepared a eulogy for him. Thus began a tradition, which continues to this day, of my preparing and delivering eulogies for all family members and close friends that have died.

In 1969 when the Americans landed on the moon, I remember trying to explain it to my mother "They're just telling you stories", she said, completely convinced in her disbelief.

Chapter 56

By the early 70's, there were quite a few Moroccan Jews living in Los Angeles, some of whom I knew from my years in Morocco. Many initially settled on the West Side, but eventually moved to the San Fernando Valley, where homes were more affordable and the schools were highly rated. Of those that lived in the Valley, somehow they all settled within a few miles of my house on Aetna Street. After so many years isolated from family and friends in Italy, it was a pleasure to have both nearby.

Though there were many synagogues throughout the city, there was no Sephardic synagogue in the Valley, and no Moroccan synagogues anywhere in Los Angeles. The Moroccan community was therefore scattered amongst several synagogues, mostly on the West Side, far from where we lived. There were a few Sephardic temples on the West Side, but they did not feel familiar because the chants were different than the ones we knew. I attended services at a Sephardic synagogue in Ladera Heights about 20 miles away, too far to go for regular services.

I remember being at the synagogue on Yom Kippur in October 1973 when a coalition of Arab states, led by Egypt and Syria, launched a joint surprise attack on Israel. We were all extremely concerned and left the temple to watch the news at the Castiel home not far from the synagogue.

Two months later on December 31, 1973 a well known and beloved member of our community, Rachel Perez, passed away. During the *Shiva* week (7 days of mourning), Moroccans from throughout Los Angeles came to the Perez home to pay their respects. Inspired by seeing all these Moroccans gathered in one place, I approached Joseph Bouzaglou, my childhood friend, and suggested that we were now numerous enough to start a temple of our own in the Valley. It turns out this idea had been on his mind for a long time. Albert Bouhadana, who joined in the discussion, was also very enthusiastic. He invited a small group of friends to meet at his home the following evening to further discuss the project.

In addition to Joe Bouzaglou, Albert Bouhadana and myself, that first meeting was attended by Leon Perez (Rachel Perez' son), Arlette Marvin (Mrs. Perez' niece) Henry Elkouby, Edmond Levy, Sarita Bouhadana and Marc Soussan. That evening, we organized a small committee and elected officers. Joe Bouzaglou was designated as our first President, I was named Treasurer, Arlette Marvin was General Secretary and Sarita Bouhadana was the Sisterhood President. The others present became the newly formed Board of Directors. We later solicited Salomon Benchetrit to join the group as our first Cantor because of his extensive knowledge of Hebrew and his experience in the singing of our ancient Sephardic melodies. Salomon Levy and Salomon Perez also joined the group and became a valuable part of our religious committee. We all agreed that it was of great importance to preserve the richness of our Sephardic heritage for our children, and everyone had the determination and sincerity to make this project a long term commitment.

Just weeks after that first meeting, we organized our first Shabbat service in a small room made available to us by Temple Adat Ariel, where we used a borrowed *Sifrei Torah* and prayed for our ultimate goal -- our own synagogue.

As word of our efforts spread and our congregation grew in number, the difficulties increased ten-fold. We had no permanent home, no rabbi and no funds. We continued to improvise as best we could, using rental halls and empty retail stores for our Shabbat services. A small hairdressing salon on Laurel Canyon became our first sanctuary. Suggested by Edmond Levy, the name Em Habanim (meaning "mother of children") was adopted.

To raise critically needed funds, we celebrated the first *Mimouna* in Los Angeles at the Adat Ariel Social Hall. It was a great success; Moroccans came from as far away as San Diego to celebrate this traditional event. We raised $3,000 that evening, which strengthened our resolve to continue.

Our first Rabbi was Jacob Dahan, who was well liked and well versed in Moroccan liturgy. Since we were on a shoestring budget Rabbi Dahan, who contributed so much in those early years, was paid very little. Over the next few years our financial position improved a bit. With the help of some very generous congregation members who guaranteed a bank loan, we purchased an old three bedroom house at 12052 Califa Street (corner of Laurel Canyon) in North Hollywood. This house was the home of Em Habanim for the next five years, during which time several other Moroccan friends joined us, all anxious to have a synagogue of our own.

Countless hours were spent in often heated and contentious debate, deciding whether to modify the old house or build something new. In addition to financial considerations, one large stumbling block was the requirement in the City Code to have a certain number of parking spaces, which was an issue due to our small lot. We eventually decided that we could not have the synagogue we really wanted in the existing structure.

12052 Califa Street, home to Em Habanim for 5 years, 1970's

In January 1984, ten years after that first meeting at Albert Bouhadana's house, work on Em Habanim's permanent home began. The completion and inauguration of the Sanctuary in October 1984 was greeted with festivities and joy. Rabbi Shimon Marciano, a devoted friend of the temple and a generous donor, put the mezuzah on the door of the new Sanctuary, which is now named after him. Rabbi Samuel Ohana also played a significant role in the evolution of Em Habanim as an advisor and committee member for several years.

It did not take long for us to realize that we needed an even larger space. Attendance had increased substantially, along with requests for children's study classes, special events etc. The recruitment of Rabbi Haim Louk further enhanced Em Habanim's reputation as an important Sephardic institution. We were thus faced with an urgent need to expand our existing facilities to an adjacent empty lot which had been acquired a few years earlier and had been fully paid for by very generous congregants.

The expansion plans included building what is now our Social Hall. Once again, parking was a major stumbling block, which was resolved when we entered into an agreement for additional parking spaces with the church across the street.

The ambitious project required tremendous financial support and all the congregants participated. In addition, we were able to secure a large loan with the help of my brother André, who was named Comptroller for Em Habanim and remains so to this day.

Em Habanim recently celebrated its 40th anniversary. Under the leadership of Rabbi Joshua Bittan, the synagogue has continued to thrive. Joshua has been associated with Em Habanim since the early days of the temple, having served on various committees and as a past president. He comes from a family of prominent rabbis in Morocco and was encouraged by me and others in the congregation to become a Rabbi because of his extensive knowledge of Hebrew and his devotion to our synagogue. Rabbi Bittan and Cantor Shimon Sibony are to be congratulated for their continued efforts to preserve our special Moroccan liturgies and traditions so that the American-born youth can carry on the wonderful heritage of their Moroccan parents.

Em Habanim today, 2014

I am extremely proud of what has been accomplished at Em Habanim through the years and am grateful to all of those that have so generously given their time and money. The success of this endeavor is due to the faith, courage and commitment displayed by many. My only regret is that my parents did not live to see it. In the earliest days of the synagogue, they had been ecstatic to know that we were engaged in creating our own house of prayers. Unfortunately, they both passed away before we broke ground on the Sanctuary. Their original (now restored) 103 year old *Ketubah* currently hangs in the foyer of our Social Hall, so they are forever a part of Em Habanim.

Chapter 57

In 1974 while I was working for L.A District Corps of Engineers, a vacancy opened up due to the retirement of the District Security Officer. The job required technical and managerial experience in directing the security of a large organization. The successful applicant would serve as a staff member and advisor to the Commander.

The pay grade for the security position was higher than mine, and I figured that if I could get that job combined with mine, it would not only make a difference in terms of my pay, but would also increase my value to the organization. So I approached my boss with the suggestion to merge the security duties with my existing responsibilities. I told him that during my youth in Morocco I had worked for a U.S. legal office where my duties included some of those performed by the retiring employee. I felt competent to do the job and was willing to be trained in a Military facility. By giving me the additional responsibilities, I argued, the Corps could save the full salary of the retiring employee.

Normally a job of this caliber would be filled by announcing the position throughout the Federal offices. However, my boss was receptive to my idea and postponed the recruitment. I was sent to a Military Police School in Aniston, Alabama for three weeks of training where I learned to develop plans for security protection from threats, sabotage, crime and other emergency conditions. The main focus of the training was the protection of flood control channels and large dams in the Southwest United States.

I graduated from the training program and became a Security and Law Enforcement Officer, certified by the U.S. Defense Department. Shortly thereafter, a Lieutenant Colonel that I had become friendly with made me an honorary member of the U.S. Military Police.

As a Security and Law Enforcement Officer, I was in charge of security for about a dozen dams in California, Arizona and Nevada and would visit them annually. I was also the investigating officer for issues related to dam employees and would prepare reports on any missing equipment or crimes within the dam sites. In addition, I worked closely with the Los Angeles Police Department when crimes were committed within the downtown District building where I worked.

These Law Enforcement duties were in addition to my regular administrative duties. I also served as Classified Documents Manager, which involved sensitive clearances for personnel assigned to the District. I worked with the FBI and the OCE (Office of the Chief of Engineers) in Washington to ensure that potential Corps employees didn't have anything in their background that would preclude them from having access to highly classified documents.

One of the most difficult assignments I had as a security officer was when I had to cancel the security clearance of a U.S. Army Lieutenant Colonel. I felt terrible because this officer was a friend with whom I often went out to lunch. He had always commended my work and had presented me with many awards, including monetary bonuses. This officer was eventually fired, then arrested. It turns out that during the Vietnam War, he had assumed the identity of a dead soldier.

During my 40 years with the Corps (including my years in Morocco), I rose from a GS4 pay grade to a GS14, which is equivalent to a Lieutenant Colonel. (The top level in my District was GS15). I was familiar with all the U.S. Army regulations related to my functions including communications, travel, supplies, security, etc. I made it my business to become indispensable. All the high ranking officers knew who I was and often called upon me to assist them when questions arose regarding Army rules and regulations. I received hundreds of commendations throughout my career for superior job performance. I have included a few of these at the end of this book (see pages 194 - 199).

* * * * * * * * * *

In July 1976, my Los Angeles office was called upon to provide support for the relocation of the Mediterranean Division from Italy to its new headquarters in Winchester, VA. I was selected to assist in the relocation of several hundred employees, military equipment, vehicles, and massive amounts of records, as well as developing working procedures for the new Division. This task required a five week absence from Los Angeles, so Juliette and 12 yr old Sandi accompanied me to Virginia.

Our hotel was about twenty miles from the base in the Blue Ridge Mountains. The drive to work was absolutely spectacular, like a painting of vivid colors from oak, maple, birch and hardwood trees in full bloom.

It was great to be reunited with many coworkers and friends we had known in Italy, particularly Henry Sibony and his family. Henry had stayed in Italy for twenty years, twice as long as we had. His children spoke Italian fluently, while mine had started to forget a little.

We visited many sites in Washington, DC including the Smithsonian, the Ford Theater (where Lincoln was assassinated), the Capitol, the White House etc. Upon my return I was honored to receive a beautiful letter of appreciation for the work I did on this assignment.

Chapter 58

On the evening of January 15, 1977 I received a frantic call from my mother Simha. My father had fallen on the bathroom floor and was not responding. I immediately called the paramedics and rushed to the apartment, just five minutes away.

As I rode with him in the ambulance, he was breathing and his eyes were open, but he could not speak. I noticed a tear in his eye, as if he was aware of what was happening. The doctor said he had suffered a massive stroke, resulting in paralysis of half his body. Shortly after arriving at the hospital, his vital body functions ceased and he passed away gently at the age of 85. After he passed, my mother said "When we lose a father or a mother, it is like a crown that drops from our heads and we are no longer the same".

My Dad loved the U.S. and was very happy to be surrounded by his children. Though he was not a demonstrative man, we all knew the tremendous pride he had for his family. His humility, great sense of humor and pride for his family were traits passed on to his children, and he will live in our hearts forever.

My sister Esther was quite involved in caring for our aging parents. After losing her husband Elie Elbaz, she lived with and assisted them in every way possible.

Two years after my father died, my mother Simha became ill. She had always been in good health, but the loss of her husband marked her profoundly. In the spring of 1979 after she attended her granddaughter Suzanne Elbaz' wedding, she became very weak. Nevertheless, she continued to hold special *Dafina* lunches for the family every Saturday and took great pride in her daily prayers and attendance at synagogue services.

Simha's was a magical woman full of love and charm; her smile could lighten a heavy heart. Many Moroccan friends adored her, particularly the way she would greet them when they visited her. She would often tell me to never hold a grudge. In fact, if someone was not speaking to her, she would cross the street to talk to them, and would say "I don't know why you don't talk to me. Please forgive me if I caused you any sadness." She loved people and was always willing to help those in need. When my siblings and I would give her some money so she could buy something special for herself, she would instead send that money to a needy sister in Israel.

I was at work when I received the call to rush to the hospital, where her condition had worsened. She died while I was still on the freeway. The date was June 7, 1979, and she was 84 years old. She was our shining star and we all miss her terribly.

My parents Judah and Simha, 1950's

My mother Simha, 1970's

Chapter 59

In October 1979 I had the honor and great privilege to be selected by the Corps of Engineers Headquarters in Washington DC to be a member of a forward group of Engineers and other key personnel sent to Israel to establish an office in Tel Aviv to be called NEPO (Near East Project Office).

In September 1978, Israelis and Egyptian negotiators met with U.S. President Jimmy Carter to negotiate the terms of a peace accord. An agreement was signed in March 1979 which called for the phased withdrawal of all Israeli troops from the Sinai by 1982. The Camp David Accords included an American pledge to build two Air Bases in the Negev (Ovda and Mitzpe Ramon), and a period of three years was delineated for the completion of these bases. NEPO was to serve as the coordinator for the building of the bases.

One of the clauses in the initial contract was that no Israeli firm be required to work on this project since they were all, at the time, quite busy doing work for Iran. However when the Shah of Iran was removed and Khomeini took power, all the Israeli firms were expelled from Iran. As a result, the Israeli government insisted that the hiring of foreign firms be stopped so that Israeli firms returning from Iran could be hired instead.

My main function consisted of providing technical and logistical support in administrative and security areas. My office was located on the top floor of the IBM building in the center of Tel Aviv. The view of the city from my office was breathtaking -- the deep blue of the Mediterranean contrasted with the white city.

Juliette accompanied me on this assignment and we spent five weeks in Tel Aviv at the Sheraton Hotel on Ben Yehuda Street. The night we arrived, the entire city was under curfew. An Israeli bus had been attacked by terrorists the day before and several people had been killed. The Sheraton was very close to where the bus had been bombed, so Israeli soldiers with machine guns were guarding the hotel's main entrance.

The hotel was fully occupied by U.S. personnel so there was heavy security was everywhere and we were accompanied to our room with flashlights. After the thirteen hour flight from Los

Angeles, we were so exhausted that we slept with our clothes on. Juliette was a bit scared about the situation and had second thoughts about being there, but changed her mind the next morning when she opened the curtains and saw the magnificent view of a beautiful beach and the endlessly blue sea.

One of the perks offered for U.S. personnel was a free private vehicle to visit the country on weekends, however there was a long waiting list to get a car. Lucky for us, the hotel clerk in charge of the motor pool happened to be from Casablanca. Because I was there on a temporary assignment, he placed my name on top of the list and I was quickly assigned a Peugeot 404 for the duration of my stay. I liked that car so much that I sought out and purchased the same one upon my return to the United States.

Having the car enabled us to visit relatives in Jerusalem, Ashdod, Ber Sheva and other towns. We loved Israel, its food, its weather and above all the camaraderie that existed within Tsahal Army soldiers who were so proud and determined to defend their country. Their spirit made us feel so proud to be Jewish.

We spent Rosh Hashanah and Yom Kippur with relatives in Jerusalem and Ashdod which was an unforgettable experience. What was also remarkable was that I was able to recite a *kaddish* in Israel for my mother. She had died few months prior to this trip and her desire was to be buried in Israel. (We decided to bury her in Los Angeles next to my father who had passed two years earlier). So to be able to say a *kaddish* for her in Israel was very significant and to this day, I marvel at the confluence of events that brought me to Israel at that precise time, like a divine hand had directed me.

Prior to leaving Israel, I was personally thanked for my work by a three star general of the U.S. Air Force, which was quite an honor. (The Corps was managing the project for the US Air Force).

Our return flight was to stop in Paris, where we planned to spend a few days, then fly on to Strasbourg. The plane sat on the tarmac in Tel Aviv for forty five minutes, with the passengers wondering what was going on. Then we heard sirens and a big limousine pulled up with a police escort and a group of passengers emerged from the car. "These must be important people", I thought.

Juliette and I were sitting just a few rows from first class, so I peeked through the separation curtain to see who was coming in. I told Juliette I saw a gentleman with an eye patch who appeared to be Moshe Dayan! (Mr. Dayan, an Israeli war hero who was instrumental in the Camp David peace accord with Egypt, was now the Foreign Minister of Israel.)

During the flight I told Juliette that I was going to talk to Moshe Dayan. "You wouldn't dare" she said. "Just watch me," I replied. So I got up from my seat and walked toward the first class area, where three huge security guys stopped me. I explained that I was very honored to be on the same flight as such an important man, and that we had a connection because his wife Rachel was my nephew's fiancée's aunt. (Dennis Karmazyn was engaged to a young woman named Roseanne, whose mother is Rachel Dayan's sister.) Amazingly, they allowed me through the curtain and I spent about fifteen minutes talking with Moshe and Rachel Dayan, who were headed to Strasbourg for an important conference. Mr. Dayan asked me about the NEPO project and thanked me for my efforts.

As I returned to my seat, in awe and disbelief over who I had just been taking to, I remember thinking that he did not look well. Moshe Dayan died of cancer two years later.

Chapter 60

The Federal Executive Board's mission is to strengthen the management and administration of Federal activities with the objective of improving intergovernmental coordination, cost-reduction and to better serve the public. The Los Angeles District of the Corps of Engineers, being a senior agency in the L.A. Federal Building, was designated as the lead agency on the program and I was chosen as the official representative for the Corps and named Chairman of the Federal Blood Bank Program.

This program involved 6,000 employees from various government agencies located in the Los Angeles downtown area. In coordination with the American Red Cross and with the assistance of various managers from all agencies, I was in charge of managing and directing the two annual blood drives held at the Federal Building, where we would collect between 200 and 300 pints of blood. I was in that position for 19 years starting in the 70s. I was very proud to work on this important program and received many awards from high-ranking Army officials and from the local Red Cross.

As a member of the Federal Executive Board, I was also designated as the Chairman of the Combined Federal Campaign which included the March of Dimes, a program to collect funds for handicapped children. I managed the Campaign for 10 consecutive years (1974-1984). I received two Commanders awards for Civilian Service and was nominated twice as a "Distinguished Employee" by the Federal Executive Board. In one of the ceremonies, I was delighted to receive my award from Bob Hope himself.

At work in the 1980's

Chapter 61

The early 1980s were a time of tense relations between the U.S. and the Soviet Union. The Soviet occupation of Afghanistan brought trade and cultural embargoes from the United States and highly visible gestures such as the United States' boycott of the 1990 Summer Olympics in Moscow. When Mikhail Gorbachev became General Secretary in March 1985 things eased up a little and contacts increased between the two superpowers.

In 1986 a group of high level U.S. Military personnel was invited to attend meetings in Moscow with their Soviet counterparts. Among this group was an Army General who represented the Corps of Engineers. The General arrived in Los Angeles on a Thursday evening and spent the night at the home of my Commanding officer, Colonel Fred Butler.

Early on Friday morning, I received a call at my office from Colonel Butler to report to his office immediately. I was told that because the visiting General had not secured an entry visa from the Russian Embassy in Washington, it was necessary to obtain that visa from the Russian Consulate in San Francisco (there was no Russian Consulate in Los Angeles at that time). There was no time to waste, the Colonel said. "Sid, take the General's passport to the Russian Consulate and get the necessary visa. You can use my driver to get to the Burbank Airport for the 9 am flight. You need to return *today* with the visa since he is leaving for Russia tonight".

When I arrived in San Francisco a little after 10:00 am, a government car was waiting to take me to the Russian Consulate. At the Consulate, I introduced myself and explained the purpose of my visit: It was extremely important to obtain a visa for the General as he was due to depart from Los Angeles that same evening. "It is impossible to deliver a visa on such a short notice" I was told. Since I could not return empty handed, I respectfully told them that I was not going to budge from the Consulate until they made the necessary contacts with their higher ups in Washington and provided me with the visa.

I waited for hours while the Consulate personnel made frantic calls to their superiors. When I wanted to use the restroom, they had an escort accompany me. It was close to 4pm when I finally obtained the visa stamp on the General's passport. I took the next available flight back and delivered the passport about 7:30pm.

I was warmly received at the office and congratulated for my successful effort. At a staff meeting the next Monday, Colonel Butler mentioned how resourceful I was and told the story about the Russian restroom escort, which made everyone laugh.

Chapter 62

On October 17, 1989 I attended a retirement seminar for government employees in San Francisco. Juliette accompanied me on this trip so we could spend a few days visiting our daughters Sandi (who was living there at the time) and Josiane, as well as Josiane's daughter Briana, who was 8 months old at the time.

After the seminar, I went to meet Juliette, who had Briana with her, at a retail store in Union Square. Once at the store, Juliette asked me to keep an eye on Brianna's stroller while she went to the fitting room to try on a sweater. As I stood there, a sudden and violent shaking occurred and the entire floor was swaying, which felt like being on a rollercoaster. I knew it was an earthquake. The lights went out and the entire building continued to shake, with fixtures and merchandise flying everywhere. We rushed outside, with Juliette still wearing the unpaid new sweater and me frantic about Briana's safety.

Union Square was filled with a cloud of dust and shattered glass from the broken windows of a nearby Macys Department store. The scene was frightening as a large number of people exiting various buildings were rushing right and left, not knowing where to go. I saw some people rush into a nearby bar -- I guess they needed a drink! Phone lines were jammed as people tried to reach their loved ones (there were no cell phones at the time) and rumors were circulating about what had and had not been damaged.

When I heard there was a major fire in the Marina District, I panicked since Josiane lived near there. I wanted to get to Josiane's as quickly as possible, but we had no car and had Briana in the stroller. Then I saw one, lone taxi coming down the street while honking his horn. I stood in the middle of the street, forcing the taxi to stop. Though there was already a passenger in the car, I opened the door to the back seat and shoved the stroller inside. "This baby needs to eat and her mother lives only three blocks from here", I said. The taxi driver agreed to take us and the other passenger also. Little did they know that Josiane lived about twelve blocks from Union Square. Josiane's house was fine and she was very relieved to see us.

We learned by radio the extent of the damage. A section of the Bay Bridge had collapsed and; the top deck of freeway 880 had dropped to the lower section, flattening several cars. Abandoning our things at the Union Square hotel for now, we stayed with Josiane for the next few days, gathering news by the minute. My youngest daughter Sandi was also with us.

Since there was no power, all the hotels took their frozen items and placed them on tables in the streets, free for the taking. Eventually we would learn that the 7.8 magnitude tremor caused 63 deaths and over 3,000 injuries, as well as $524 million in property damage. We considered ourselves very lucky to be alive.

The rest of the retirement seminar was cancelled. However, because of the harrowing experience, I was determined to prepare myself for an eventual retirement, understanding that even the best laid plans could be thwarted by Mother Nature. One year later I opted to retire from Government service .

Chapter 63

During my long career with the Army Corps of Engineers, I was constantly learning, attending classes and seminars whenever I could. I learned how to set priorities and clearly articulate project goals so my team would know how to proceed, identifying each member's role and creating a shared sense of responsibility in the outcome.

It was with this same approach that I decided to retire in November 1990. After many conversations with my "team" (Juliette and my three daughters), we all agreed it was time for me to focus on other interests. I was 65 years old, had 40 years of continuous service, and was eligible to receive a lump sum of money as well as a significant pension.

Still, leaving the Corps was not an easy decision. Working for the Corps was a formative and defining experience for me, allowing me to further my education and exposing me to important projects at home and abroad. In retrospect, I made the right decision because it allowed me to spend eighteen years of quality time with my cherished wife before her passing in 2008.

On the day I retired, a special luncheon was organized by the staff in my honor and I was presented with a book that had been signed by all district employees (there were hundreds), from the lowest level clerk to Generals. Each of them praised and thanked me for my service. I was deeply moved and immensely proud of their comments. They had been like family to me and I will never forget their kindness and friendship.

I had invited my three daughters to attend this luncheon and was upset that they all declined. Little did I know that they were busy planning their own celebration for me. Taking advantage of the fact that many relatives from Paris and Montreal were in Los Angeles for a family wedding, they had the whole family (siblings, nieces and nephews) gather at my house for a surprise party.

Everyone was dressed in Army attire. I was moved to tears at this special gathering in my honor and was further surprised the next day when presented with a video where each of my relatives expressed his/her ideas regarding what I should do after my retirement. I considered myself a very lucky man to have such a great family. Knowing that I would be surrounded with their affection and love for years to come made the thought of retiring easier to handle.

One year after retiring I received a letter from the Corps stating that, in recognition for my "distinguished and exceptional service", I had been selected for inclusion in the Los Angeles District Gallery of Distinguished Civilian Employees. This was a tremendous honor since there less than twenty names in this Gallery from the thousands of employees who have worked for the Federal

Government in Los Angeles. There was an induction ceremony, followed a few weeks later by the hanging of a gold plaque, with my name and years of service in the conference room of the Corps offices on Wilshire Blvd., where it remains to this day. I believe I am the only foreign born person to have received this honor.

With Juliette at my retirement luncheon, 1990

Chapter 64

It was with great joy that Juliette and I celebrated the weddings of our daughters.

Josiane - San Francisco 1987

Josiane met Joseph Feigon in San Francisco when she was 28 years old and he was 30. Set up by a mutual friend, it was a match made in heaven. Everyone called them Joe and Jo.

Joseph came from a well-educated, middle class, Ashkenazi family who was thrilled to have Josiane add some spice to their family. The Feigons hosted a large engagement party at their home in Aptos, CA and a few days later the traditional Moroccan Henna was held on October 17th at El Mansour Moroccan Restaurant. Josiane wore "La Grande Robe", a hand-made, traditional Moroccan dress which was first worn by my mother as her wedding dress. This priceless family treasure is now over 100 years old has been worn by many of the Chriqui women on the night of their Henna.

The next day was the wedding, held at the California Culinary Academy, a cooking school housed in a beautiful historical building with beaux arts interior. There were 225 guests for the formal evening wedding. For an elegant and dramatic touch, Josiane wore a white satin turban with her veil.

Josiane's marriage to Joseph lasted 15 years and produced my first beautiful granddaughter, Briana.

Colette - Santa Cruz 1988

Colette and Jim met in Santa Cruz when she was 22 years old and he was 27. After dating for 10 years, they finally decided to get married. Jim was raised in Carmel in a family of Basque and English descent. In order to marry Colette, Jim converted to Judaism.

With 150 guests in attendance, Jim and Colette got married on February 14th at the Monterey Plaza Hotel on a bluff overlooking the ocean. The Chuppah was carried in and held in place by friends and family. It was a warm, picture perfect afternoon, with the sun glistening off the Pacific. At times, the Rabbi's voice was drowned out by the sounds of the sea lions below.

Colette looked stunning in an ivory dress custom-made by her Aunt Yvonne Gabay. Jim later confessed that he couldn't wait to take off his shoes and run in the sand. That day the San Francisco Chronicle had an article on Valentine's Day weddings and prominently featured Colette and Jim's story as well as picture of the happy couple.

Colette's marriage to Jim lasted 22 years and produced my second beautiful granddaughter, Kaylie.

Sandi - Beverly Hills 1997

In September of 1995, an old family friend and member of our Moroccan community, Vicky Levy, passed away and *Shiva* services were held at her home. It was on one of those nights that Sandi met her future husband, Mike Bouhadana. Sandi and Mike had so much in common since Mike was the son of Moroccan parents who were also founders of Em Habanim. Sandi was living in Orlando, FL at the time while Mike lived in Los Angeles. After about eight months of a long-distance relationship, they became engaged.

On September 4th, 1997 Sandi and Mike had a traditional Moroccan Henna party at the home of Mike's cousin in Beverly Hills. Sandi wore *La Grande Robe* along with a headdress from Mike's side of the family.

Three days later, Mike and Sandi were married at the Regent Beverly Wilshire Hotel in Beverly Hills. This was an elegant affair with over 250 people in attendance from all parts of the world. Instead of a first dance, Sandi opted to serenade Mike with the song "Come Rain or Come Shine".

Two years later, on August 18, 1999, their first child and my first grandson, Ethan Abraham Bouhadana was born. Abraham was Mike's father's Hebrew name, which is why they selected it. By pure coincidence, Abraham was also the Hebrew name I had chosen for Sandi when I briefly thought she would be a boy. In 2003, they had a second son, Matthew Solomon Bouhadana. In 2005, my third granddaughter was born, Ava Juliette.

Sandi and Mike have been married for 17 years and live about a mile from my house.

Josiane, Juliette, Sandi and Colette, 1987

Chapter 65

In 2006, after a routine blood test, Juliette was diagnosed with Hepatitis C. It was not clear to any of us what this meant or when/how she had contracted this virus. We soon learned that Hepatitis C is often called the "silent epidemic" because you can have the virus for years or even decades and not know it. In Juliette's case, the doctors surmised that it had been dormant for thirty or forty years and was a sort of "time bomb" in her body.

Shortly after being diagnosed, the disease began to affect Juliette's health in noticeable ways. As the incurable disease progressed, Juliette's energy levels dropped and water from her stomach moved to her lungs, requiring frequent, painful, paracentesis procedures (fluid extractions from one lung). Several types of medicine and various procedures were tried to slow the progression of the disease, to no avail. For two years she fought bravely, always hopeful that she would get better, but by mid December 2008 it became evident that the end was near.

Although we were acutely aware of the seriousness of her condition, we were still in denial and when she died and it was a shock to everyone. I was not ready to say goodbye to the love of my life and the center of our family. Neither were our daughters or Juliette's "twin" sister Yvonne. Juliette passed away on December 16th, 2008. I cannot describe the devastation and enormous grief we all felt. I experienced a complete collapse of all my senses and felt numb for days.

After the funeral when we were sitting *Shiva* at home, a sweet and emotional thing happened: my second grandson Matthew Bouhadana, not yet 6 years of age, pulled me into a corner, got his small wallet out and offered me the only money he had in it…one dollar bill, along with a big hug and a plea for me to stop crying. I understood then that even though my beloved was gone, there was still so much to live for.

September 2007

Chapter 66

As I have been writing this memoir and reflecting on my life, I am grateful for the luck and good fortune I've had, beginning with my wonderful siblings, each of whom played a significant role in shaping who I am. I have spoken about each sibling in the preceding pages, but would like to take a moment here to relate the following about each one.

Renée (1913 -2010)

A beautiful woman of many talents, Renée was generous and full of life. As the oldest of the clan, she inspired me with her strong attachment to our parents and her siblings, even after her marriage and move to another city. She frequently visited us in Casablanca and I was always happy to see her.

Renée loved music and played the piano well. She had a wonderful sense of humor and loved to laugh; her smile was infectious. Renée's superb cooking and pastry skills were legendary in Morocco and later in Canada.

With her husband Albert Dery, she had five children: Guy, Andrée (Doudou), Gabriel, Danielle and William. Both Albert and Rene have passed and are buried in Israel.

David (1914 - 2010)

There is no one quite like my brother David. One year younger than Renée, David was a handsome man with great personality and a wonderful attitude. He also loved music and studied the violin in his youth.

At a very young age he took on huge responsibilities when he assumed the role of head of the Chriqui household. I was profoundly influenced by his devotion to us and his leadership in helping raise his younger siblings. He never complained and did everything in his power to alleviate our difficult situation during the war years.

David has always had a special place in my heart because of his tireless actions to take care of me when I was gravely ill with typhoid.

With his spouse Viviane, he had four children: Claude, Delia, Evelyne and Chantal. David is buried in Montreal, Canada.

Esther (Apr 1916 -   )

Esther was a happy young woman, always singing and dancing in the house. Together with David, Esther took on the heavy burden of supporting the family, at the expense of pursuing her studies. It is thanks to Esther and David that we were able to survive. I greatly admire her commitment to caring full time for our aging parents after the passing of her husband Elie.

Esther is now 98 and I am amazed at how sharp her mind still is. She can recall events from long ago with precision. Esther now lives with her devoted daughter Suzanne and son-in-law Gilbert Rebboah in Dana Point, California. Her son Albert lives in Paris and visits often.

Claudia (1919 -2004)

From a very young age, Claudia demonstrated tremendous determination, strength and courage. She was a woman of action who was constantly looking for ways to improve our lives during the difficult WWII days in Morocco and later when she immigrated to this country.

A pioneer, she was the first in our family to come to the U.S. in 1942 at the age of 23. At a time when women did not travel unaccompanied, she embarked alone on a transatlantic journey to America in the middle of a war. She arrived in New York and, though she spoke no English and did not know how to sew, managed to get a job as a seamstress. Later in Los Angeles, after having worked for a time making curtains, she opened her own custom drapery store. That resilience and resourcefulness shaped all our lives, for she is the one who sponsored several of us to immigrate to the U.S.

I had a special relationship with Claudia and will be forever grateful for her kindness and generosity in helping me immigrate to this country, and for her love, care and attention in letting me live with her family for almost six years. It is because Claudia and Albert settled in Los Angeles that half the Chriqui family now lives in Los Angeles. Her love, dedication and great generosity is legendary in the family.

Jacques (Feb 1921 -   )

I have been close to Jacques since our days as youngsters skipping school to go to the beach. A great storyteller, Jacques is a man of action who loves life, music, travel , friends and good cuisine. A "bon vivant" and optimist with a great sense of humor, he also has a unique serenity and deep reserve of wisdom.

Jacques is the European in the family, having lived most of his life in Paris. We loved to travel together when I too was living in Europe. Jacques' humor is contagious and he always makes me laugh.

With his first wife Solange (now deceased), he had three children: Lydia, Richard and Martine. In 2006 at the age of 85 he married the lovely Rosette and they currently divide their time between Paris and Los Angeles. Now 93, he is still the life of the party.

Marie (1923 - 2006)

If I could use one word to describe Marie, it would be "Chutzpa", in the good sense of the word. Though all my sisters had tremendous strength and courage, Marie was unique by reason of her fierce determination and sheer audacity.

Marie was faced with enormous responsibilities when her husband died, leaving her with 4 young children. I believe divine intervention helped Marie as her life was changed from despair to hope to success. Who else but Marie could have a TV show bring her children to Los Angeles from Morocco? And who else but Marie could meet wonderful Elliott while hitchhiking on Valleyheart Drive? Elliot, who had no children when they met, had an instant family with Roger, Lucienne, Henry and Corinne. Marie and Elliot had two more children, Louie and Michelle. Elliot passed two years after Marie died, and both are buried in Los Angeles.

André (Apr 1929 -   )

A reflective, disciplined man, André is the quietest of my siblings. As a child he was always willing to help others, which has continued to this day. André loves music and plays the clarinet. He embodies Jewish values and is always striving to improve things for the Jewish community. It is because of his commitment and prudent financial management that Em Habanim has been able to survive and thrive. Besides being my brother, André is also a good friend and confidant.

With his dedicated wife Therese, they have three children: Kathy, Nicole and Patrick, all of whom live in Los Angeles.

Maurice (Jun 1933 -   )

The youngest in the family Maurice is also the most daring. He is full of life, joy and intense aliveness. He immigrated to the U.S. soon after I did and reveled in life in America.

A "bon vivant" like Jacques, Maurice loves to have a good time and to be surrounded by good friends. A fast learner and a great talker, Maurice has the ability to make friends wherever he goes.

With his first wife Vera, Maurice had three daughters: Lisa, Debby and Kimberly. He is now remarried to Lisette, a wonderful woman who has succeeded, much to my delight, in making him more religious.

Without exception, each one of my siblings was and is dedicated to family. The bond we share was not only instrumental in helping us survive the leaner years, but has served as a model to our children and to their children, resulting in a close knit extended family. From Simha and Judah Chriqui came nine Chriqui children, who in turn had thirty-two children. Including those who have married into the family, the Chriqui family now consists of well over one hundred people. Most live in Los Angeles and Montreal, with a few in France and in Morocco. We all look forward to the many weddings, bar mitzvots and other happy occasions when we get together. Of all the blessings in my life, my family has been the greatest blessing of all.

(left to right) Top Row: André, David, me, Jacques, Maurice.
Bottom Row: Marie, Esther, Renée, Claudia. In Los Angeles, 1992

Jacques, André, me, Maurice, David, 1970's

(left to right) Top Row: André, Marie, me, Esther, Maurice, Claudia, Jacques
(Bottom) David, Renée. In Los Angeles 1992

Esther, Marie, Renée, Claudia, 1990's

The last time all nine siblings were together, Los Angeles 2002

Chapter 67

When I retired from the Government I received a beautiful glass plaque from my trusted deputy Rosemarie Sandoval, engraved with the following message:

> *There is a miracle called "Friendship" that dwells within the heart,*
> *And you don't know how it happens or when it gets its start,*
> *But the happiness it brings you always gives you a special lift,*
> *And you realize that Friendship is God's most precious gift.*

Throughout the years I have indeed been blessed with many wonderful friends who have left footprints in my heart.

Henri Leb

I met Henri in Casablanca when I was about 12 years old, right after my long bout with typhoid. He was a red haired kid with a great smile and a big heart, the only boy among several sisters. He too was a bright student, so we were constantly discussing school work, history and world affairs. He married a beautiful and kind woman, Maya, who converted to Judaism and who was very close to Juliette. She loved Colette and would often babysit for her when we were still living in Morocco.

Henri lost his father at a young age and became head of the household. As such, he felt obligated to take care of this mother and therefore never left Morocco. When I immigrated to America, we started a regular correspondence as he was quite interested in my new country. When I returned to Morocco after being away for a year, he wanted to know every detail of my life in America. We corresponded regularly throughout my years in Los Angeles, in Italy, and back in Los Angeles. With the advent of computers, we now stay in touch via email and Skype.

About two years ago when I visited Morocco with my daughter Josiane, we stayed at Henri's house. Henri was quite successful in Real Estate and has a beautiful villa in Anfa, a wealthy seaside suburb of Casablanca. We were astonished when Henri showed us a thick binder titled "Sidney" where he kept all the correspondence and pictures he had saved since I first went to the U.S. in the 1940's. Josiane and I were very touched by this incredible testament to our friendship.

Henri Elkouby

I met Henri when we both were 12 years old. A handsome, intelligent kid, we were close from the moment the teacher made him sit next to me in class.

Like Henri Leb, Henri Elkouby became the father figure to his three sisters Vicky, Margot and Rosette when he lost his father at the age of 10. At that young age, his sisters would call him "Baba" which means Dad. Henri had to quit school in his early teens so he could work to support his family, yet he remained an avid learner, greatly interested in books and world events. He would come to my house every morning and walk with me to school before going to work so he could grill me on what I had learned the previous day. His house was full of books on every subject you could imagine.

We lost touch while I lived in Italy, but reconnected when he immigrated to Los Angeles around 1969 with his wife Aida and two sons, Alain and David. When Aida became very ill Henri was at her side day and night. The death of Aida was very traumatic for Henri and he never fully recovered from the emotional blow.

Roger Harroch - I met Roger when I was about 14 and he was 16. Like Henri Elkouby, he too was the only boy among five sisters. We had a lot in common -- he loved the parties, dancing, music etc. as much as I did. Like me, Roger also worked for the U.S. forces after they landed in Morocco. He immigrated to the U.S. with his wife Laurie during the time I was stationed in Italy, ultimately settling in San Francisco.

Though we were not in touch while I lived in Livorno, we reconnected again in the late 60's when I returned to Los Angeles. I would regularly travel to San Francisco and he to Los Angeles. After divorcing his first wife in the 80's, Roger moved to Paris where he still lives today with his second wife, Violette.

Unfortunately for the past two years we have not been in contact.

Joseph Bouzaglou

Two years older than me, Joe and I were friends since our days at the *École Industrielle*, when we were both expelled, then allowed to return. He was very bright and was always the top of his class. Our parents were very close and lived in the same area in Casablanca. Mr. Bouzaglou was very religious, as was my mother, so they would often get together to discuss religion.

Joe and I worked together for the Americans in Casablanca. He would process the paperwork for the new hires that I would interview. While I was in Italy, Joe immigrated to Cleveland, OH. In our mail correspondence, I told him he should move to Los Angeles because it was too cold in Cleveland. "But I don't know anyone in Los Angeles" was his answer. "My sister Claudia and her husband Albert live there. They will help you", I replied. So Joe took my advice and moved to Los Angeles and, as they did for so many others, Claudia and Albert helped him get settled.

As I mentioned previously, Joe was one of the founders of Em Habanim. He was a man of vision and was always at the forefront of the synagogue projects we created. He married a nice woman Marie and they had four children, Patrick, Jimmy, Sandra and Linda.

Sadly, Joe passed away three years ago and I miss him terribly. He was a man of dignity, integrity and great intelligence, and was devoted to the Community.

Henry Sibony

I met Henry Sibony in 1949 when I was on a visit to Morocco. He was about to immigrate to the U.S. and planned to live in New York. I kept telling him to come to Los Angeles instead. After a short stint in New York he moved to Los Angeles where I found him a job with a Tunisian friend, Robaire, who owned a restaurant on La Brea. I told Robaire that I had a friend who knew how to make Moroccan salads, when in fact Henry had never cooked in his life!

We stayed in touch until I left for Morocco in 1954. In 1955, after Henry became an American citizen, he traveled to Morocco and we met again in a Casablanca synagogue during the High Holidays. Henry was planning on returning to the U.S. after his visit because he had a girlfriend in Los Angeles. When I learned that his girlfriend was a non-Jewish divorcee with one child, I urged him to stay longer in Casablanca, find a nice Jewish girl and get married. By this time I was married with one daughter, and we were living in a beautiful apartment in Casablanca.

He said he had no job in Morocco so I promised to get him one. I had been working on the American base for awhile and knew they needed someone in the warehouse so I got him a job with the Corps as a warehouse man. Soon thereafter, Henry was introduced to a beautiful Moroccan girl 15 years his junior named Violette. They fell in love and were married.

In 1957, Henry was transferred to Livorno shortly before I was. Like me, Henry had three children and our families became close in Italy. Henry and Violette ended up staying in Italy for 20 years, then moved to Winchester, VA when the Corps relocated there from Livorno.

Henry retired from the Corps and now lives in Walnut Creek, CA were he enjoys a comfortable pension from the Federal Government. He has thanked me many times over the years for having changed the course of his life by convincing him to stay in Morocco back in 1955. We have stayed good friends and we frequently correspond by email.

Leon Sibony

In 1951 I had the pleasure of seeing Margot Elkouby (sister of my dear friend Henri Elkouby), when she came to Los Angeles to marry Leon Sibony. Leon's father, Sidney Sibony, was a Moroccan born entrepreneur who had left Casablanca in 1941 and had settled in Los Angeles with his wife Anita and their children Leon and Huguette, who were teenagers at the time. As an adult wanting a traditional wife, Leon had traveled to Morocco and met Margot. It was love at first sight.

They wed in Los Angeles in 1951 when Margot was about 20 years old. I was very honored to be the best man at the wedding, representing Margot's family from Morocco since she had no relatives here. I became very close to the Sibony family and mother Anita would always invite me over, particularly during the holidays. Being with that family was like being home away from home.

Leon was a very resourceful man. Having lost his dad when he was a teenager, he worked hard and was successful in many businesses, including becoming a top manager with the Cadillac Company in Encino and in Real Estate in Las Vegas. Leon died in Los Angeles several years ago, as did his mother and sister. They were all survived by Margot who now has now two grown, married children.

By incredible coincidence Margot's sister Rosette, a widow who lost her husband Joseph Chriqui (a cousin of ours) met my brother Jacques, who also was a widower. They married in Los Angeles in 2006 and now live part of the year in Paris and part of the year in Los Angeles. Rosette did not have to change her name or any monogrammed items since she married another Chriqui with the same initials !!!

Chapter 68

In every life there are golden moments that you hold in your heart forever. There were many golden moments in raising our children and no sacrifice was too great if it gave them the opportunity to better themselves. I could not be more proud of my daughters and am very pleased that they are raising their own children with the same consideration. I am quite fortunate to have five precious and beautiful grandchildren who have filled me with every wonderful experience and emotion that life has to offer.

My first two granddaughters, lovely Briana and Kaylie, each possess grace, beauty and intellect. Both are University graduates who are now in their twenties and living on their own, Briana in New York and Kaylie in Portland.

My third grandchild Ethan is a miracle child. The FIRST male born in my family, he was severely ill as an infant and has struggled with health issues throughout his young life. He is now fourteen years old, a very polite young man who loves basketball and French croissants. His middle name is Abraham, named after his paternal grandfather and Em Habanim co-founder, Albert Bouhadana. Ethan had his *Bar Mitzvah* last year and conducted himself in a brilliant manner. He is intelligent, articulate, popular and funny.

Sandi's second son Matthew is my fourth grandchild, who bears my name Salomon as his middle name. He is eleven years of age, reflective, quiet and handsome. An avid reader like me, he loves to climb and is quite good in art. He is now a Hebrew student at Em Habanim, preparing for his Bar Mitzvah.

My fifth grandchild is Ava, who's middle name is Juliette, after her grandmother. A pretty blond, blue-eyed eight year old, she is the star of the Bouhadana/Chriqui clan. She is fearless, independent and can keep up with her two older brothers at any boys' games. She loves riding horses, ballet dancing, and clothes. Like a typical girl, she loves wearing chic little outfits and cute shoes.

Of all the gifts of *Hashem*, one of the greatest is the privilege of being a grandfather. My grandchildren are extra-special and I love every one of them very dearly.

(from left) Ethan, Matthew, Kaylie, Briana, Eva, 2012

EPILOGUE

"To everything there is a season and a time for every purpose under heaven."[2]

What would a man be without his capacity to remember? Memory is a passion no less powerful or universal than love. What does it mean to remember? It is to live in more than one world. It is to prevent the past from fading and to call upon the future to illuminate it. It is to revive fragments of existence, to rescue lost beings, to cast light on past events and to drive back the sands that obscure the face of things.

It was challenging to return to long forgotten events that shaped my destiny but when I started writing and focusing on my past, a flood of memories, including precise dates of events, came back to me. I was pleasantly surprised at the thoughts and emotions that these memories evoked.

Throughout my life, one of my driving forces has been the thirst for knowledge. Even today I am still learning new things, including how to cook. Juliette was a wonderful cook, but she didn't let me step foot in the kitchen, other than to eat. She would be amazed to see me preparing many of the Moroccan dishes she used to make. Actually, I'm quite amazed myself!

The more I wrote, the more aware I became of how truly fortunate I have been. I had an interesting, rewarding career that allowed me to constantly learn and expand my horizons. I traveled extensively and continue to do so, for the possibilities are endless when you travel: to reflect on yourself, to meet new people, to learn and share experiences.

I have preserved my Jewish heritage and have been very involved in my community. This year marks the 40th anniversary of Em Habanim. I am so proud to have been a part of the synagogue since the days when it was nothing more than an idea. My continued involvement has kept me engaged since my retirement and has given me an opportunity to greatly improve my Hebrew and knowledge of the Torah.

---

[2] Ecclesiastes, Chapter 3, Verse 1

Most important in my life has been my family, starting with my siblings. In both good times and bad, the nine of us have always been there for each other. To have been married for 55 years to the love of my life was a special blessing. My gratitude goes to my wife who left me a legacy of three loving, caring and responsible daughters who constantly surround me with affection. My five grandchildren are a great source of joy and with them in my life, I will never grow old. And of course, my extended family of nieces, nephews and cousins. It is with pride that I have become the de facto Historian of this large and wonderful family.

My goal in writing this memoir was to give something of lasting value to my family and friends everywhere. I sincerely hope I have accomplished that task.

DEPARTMENT OF THE ARMY
LOS ANGELES DISTRICT, CORPS OF ENGINEERS
P.O. BOX 2711
LOS ANGELES, CALIFORNIA 90053-2325

November 30, 1990

REPLY TO
ATTENTION OF

Office of the
District Engineer

Mr. Sidney Chriqui
13048 Aetna Street
Van Nuys, California 91401

Dear Sid:

As you retire from your position as Information Management Officer, I wish to express my appreciation for your more than 40 years of loyal and faithful service. You are indeed to be commended on an exceptionally full and fruitful career in the Federal service.

A check of history shows that you started your long career after the landing of U.S. Forces in North Africa in 1943. You served with the Air Transport Command where you settled claims against the U.S. Government, worked as interpreter/translator in French and Arabic for the Judge Advocate, and assisted in the hiring of thousands of local personnel for the Command.

Your fine career with the Corps began in 1954 with the East Atlantic District in Nouasseur, Morocco, during the crash construction of U.S. Air Bases in that country. You made valuable contributions in the relocation of that District to Livorno, Italy. There you provided outstanding logistical support to personnel and property movements from Libya, Greece, Turkey, and France for what was to become the Mediterranean Division. With that office you played a significant role in the selection of the first U.S. contracting firm to do multi-million construction work in Saudi Arabia.

Your dedicated service with the Los Angeles District began in 1967. You served in key positions at the executive level for 10 District Commanders. Most noteworthy, of course, was your position as Chief, Office of Administrative Services. As Chief you made outstanding contributions to our military and civil works program. Your devotion to duty, wide experience and ability to perform varied assignments won you the respect of the District staff, the South Pacific Division, Headquarters in Washington, as well as other government and local agencies.

Your professional support; as Security and Law Enforcement Manager, as Chairman of the Blood Bank for the greater Los Angeles area for 19 years, as coordinator for the Combined Federal Campaign for 10 years; has been duly recognized.

These include 10 commendations, several outstanding and sustained superior performance awards, two Commander's Awards, numerous Special Acts, and a citation from the Deputy Secretary of the Army for exemplary representation and outstanding performance of security duties in support of the XXIII Olympic Games in Los Angeles in 1984. You may reflect on your career with pride and enthusiasm.

You have not only served the District well as a leader but also as a mentor. You have developed many competent staff members through the years who are now serving in key District positions. The Los Angeles District has indeed been fortunate, and I commend you and thank you for all that you have done for the District and for the U.S. Army Corps of Engineers.

My very best wishes go with you and your wife, Juliette, for a long, healthy and happy retirement and hope you enjoy this time to the fullest.

Sincerely,

Charles S. Thomas
Colonel, Corps of Engineers
District Engineer

DEPARTMENT OF THE ARMY

SOUTH PACIFIC DIVISION, CORPS OF ENGINEERS

630 Sansome Street, Room 720

San Francisco, California 94111-2206

REPLY TO
ATTENTION OF:

CESPD-PM (340a)   29 February 1988

MEMORANDUM THRU: Commander, Los Angeles District, ATTN: CESPL-DE

FOR: Sidney Chriqui (CESPL-DE-S)

SUBJECT: Letter of Appreciation

Through the past four years you have performed the duties as Security
and Law Enforcement Manager, U.S. Army Engineer District, Los Angeles
in an extraordinary fashion. When I arrived in this command, you were
the Dean of the Division Security Managers and, in fact, frequently
served as the Division, Chief of Security and Law Enforcement in those
instances when the military chief was unavailable. Your service has
been unwavering, unselfish and totally professional. The South Pacific
Division is indebted to you.

During my tenure, I have often sought your counsel and relied upon your
wisdom and good judgment which have consistently been superlative.
Your reputation for reliability, conscientious endeavor and determination
to do the right thing have established a benchmark for the Division
in its entirety, and especially for the Security and Law Enforcement
community. The Los Angeles District has certainly benefited from your
dedicated efforts and to a large measure owes the distinct improvement
in its security posture to your hard work and high standards. During
this period of constrained resources, you have demonstrated an enviable
degree of resourcefulness and initiative to achieve superior results.
The District's accomplishments in the security arena are directly attributable
to your diligence, pragmatism and superb leadership.

On behalf of the Division, and particularly my office, I want to express
our collective and my personal gratitude for your contribution to the
national security. Your service is characterized by honor, dignity,
integrity and a commitment to excellence which is truly representative
of the standards to which all Americans should aspire. You are credit
to your District, this Division, the Corps of Engineers, U.S. Army and
most importantly to your nation.

JOHN RACKOVAN
LTC, MP
Chief, Security and Law Enforcement
Office

February 14, 1986

Mr. Sidney Chriqui
Department of the Army
Corps of Engineers LA District
P.O. Box 2711
Los Angeles, CA   90053

Dear Sid:

I could not resist writing you one last time to say again what an
outstanding job I think you did as your agency's campaign leader in the
1985-86 CFC campaign.

We have continued to astound the non-government sector of Los Angeles and
the other major CFC's in the country. The major business community
campaigners, particularly those running the United Way campaign, cannot
believe what you have accomplished. Talk about setting the pace and
obtaining a positive image about federal employees, you certainly did it.

Today we closed the campaign books and sent the final financial report to
OPM. Would you believe $3,306,470!! That's just slightly under an 18%
increase over last year. The first year it was 14%, then 21% last year,
now 18%. I really almost do not know how you did it. I say "almost"
because after knowing you I have a good hint as to why you were so
successful.

By the way, San Francisco and Baltimore raised $2.6M and $2.7M
respectively. You polished them off real good.

You have every reason to be proud of yourself. You certainly earned my
respect and that of everyone who has heard of this achievement. Most
important, though, you have made great things happen for your community.
For that I thank you with all my heart.

I hope to see you at our last Campaign Cabinet meeting on February 18. If
not, best wishes for another outstanding campaign next year.

With personal regards,

Fred W. Bowen, Chairman
Combined Federal Campaign
Federal Executive Board

Photo by Charles Frank

Sidney Chriqui

OAS chief gets Commander's Award

The Commander's Award for Civilian Service has been presented to **Sidney Chriqui** for his work as chairman of the Los Angeles District's Combined Federal Campaign for 10 consecutive years.

Chriqui, Office of Administrative Services chief, was cited for his "exceptional planning ability, organizational acumen, personal inspiration, and undaunted dedication that enabled the District to exceed its campaign goal in each of the 10 years (1974-1984)."

He was further cited by Col. Fred Butler, District commander, for his participation as a leader in the L.A. Campaign Coordinating Committee which contributed to the success of the campaign throughout the city.

The L.A. Combined Federal Campaign, an annual fund-raising event for all area federal workers, provides the most comprehensive grouping of human care services of any metro jurisdiction in the U.S.

As District CFC chairman, Chriqui extends thanks to all LAD employees and key workers for their "wholehearted support" during the 10 years he's been involved with CFC. He is looking forward to their continued support during the October-November '85 fund drive.

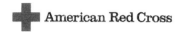 **American Red Cross**

Los Angeles Chapter
1200 South Vermont Avenue
Los Angeles, California 90006
(213) 384-5261

September 8, 1980

Dear Mr. Chriqui:

On behalf of the American Red Cross and the Los Angeles
Dodgers, this is to express my heartfelt appreciation to
you for participating as our guest at Red Cross Blood Donor
Day on September 1 at Dodger Stadium.

As a token of our gratitude, we hope that the enclosed
picture will serve as a lasting momento of the event. The
Red Cross, in its 99-year history as a voluntary organization, has continued its service to the community with
the assistance of persons like yourself who have donated
valuable time in the spirit of volunteerism.

Your effort in giving as either a blood donor or blood
services volunteer has already proved a vital link in
keeping with the needs of the community, and in bolstering
Red Cross Blood Services Program.

Having you as our guest, in conjunction with the Los Angeles
Dodgers, was our way of saying "Thanks" for donating your
time and services without asking anything in return. We
hope that the 30,000-plus in attendance at the Labor Day
game appreciated your being there as much as we did, and
we look forward to your continued involvement with Red
Cross Blood Services.

Cordially yours,

Mike Harris
Office of Public Relations

Mr. Sid Chriqui
U.S. Army Corps of Engineers
300 N. Los Angeles St.
P.O. Box 2711
Los Angeles, California 90053

Art Deco Casablanca

by Tahir Shah, Jan 26, 2012 (see www.tahirshah.com)

Stroll down the long palm-lined Boulevard Mohammed V, the heart of old Casablanca, and you have to squint to appreciate the glory of it all. On the surface it may appear more than a little frayed at the edges but look beyond the obvious, and you slip into a Twilight Zone of utter enchantment.

Laid out by the French a century ago, the old crumbling downtown was once a showcase of imperial might, one of the first cities planned by aeroplane. A gleaming jewel of Art Deco style, pre-War Casablanca was synonymous with all that was dazzling, exciting, and new. Back then, the chic restaurants and cafés were packed with men in trilbies (a narrow-brimmed type of hat once viewed as the rich man's favored hat), their women in long silk gloves and heels. These days, a façade of grime may cover every surface, but the magic's still there, waiting to be revealed. And more to the point, change is afoot. The phoenix is about to rise from the flames once again.

A stone's throw from the Central Market, a farrago of fresh fish and hopeful cats, a pair of wizened old *pied noir* take coffee on the pavement outside Le Petit Poucet. The syrupy morning North African light bathing them in shadows, they reminisce of how things used to be.

"They all came here to dine," growls François, his voice roughened from a lifelong love affair with Gauloises. "Among them, Albert Camus, Saint-Exupéry and Edith Piaf." "In the twenties and thirties, the greatest architects flooded to Casablanca," adds Laurent. "They worked with a blank canvas, creating a cultural masterpiece!" Across from him, François sips his coffee and scowls. "The city was in full bloom back then. It was a fragment of paradise.""So what happened?" I asked. The Frenchman frowns at the question, as the ancient waiter shuffles forwards with fresh glasses of ubiquitous café noir. "Independence! That's what happened. And, all of a sudden, this precious *bijou* was thrown into the trash!

In the seven years I have lived in Casablanca, I've discovered the secret Art Deco splendor and understated opulence. The grandeur is everywhere....in the details. Amble through the backstreets off the main boulevard, and you can't help but notice it. The marble foyers are adorned with the finest quality brass-work, parquet, and wrought-iron, the curved lettering outside each building hinting at a time when Casablanca was wealthy in the extreme.

There's a sense that this wasn't just another city, but a statement. The French constructed every inch with abounding national pride. But despite the grand pedigree, modern Casablanca has lost its identity and the glorious city has paid a heavy price.

With their sleek curved lines, cupolas, and floral motifs, the majestic old apartment blocks of Mers Sultan are as impressive as anything you might find at Miami Beach. Once a posh residential quarter, Mers Sultan is a treasure trove of buildings that are the epitome of faded grandeur. My favorite is the Café Champs Elysée, a great rollicking rollercoaster of a building, fashioned in the shape of a luxury cruise liner.

Nearby, across from the Art Deco Cinema Lynx, is the iconic Bar Atomic. Dating from the thirties, when anything with the word 'atomic' in the title was regarded as cutting edge, it's one of a kind. Behind the bar, the bottles of cheap Flag Special beer are kept cool in the original wooden fridges, the speckled granite floor hidden beneath a layer of sawdust.

Many of the old Art Deco villas are being demolished, reduced to rubble by teams of men with sledge hammers. The fixtures and fittings end up in a junkyard in Hay Hasseni. I spend a lot of time there, trawling through the wreckage, hunting for gems. I you go often enough, you can find roll-top baths with claw feet, wooden roller blinds, and fabulous washbasins the size of cattle troughs. But each cluster of baths discovered means another magnificent Art Deco villa has been torn down.

But the green shoots of recovery are all around. With the backing of the king, there's a grand plan to revitalize the old heart of Casablanca, just before it ceases to beat. A tramway is being constructed, expected to be launched next year. It will link the main thoroughfare Mohammed V to other areas of the city. After all, one of the great problems has been that the post-Colonial centre moved away to the chic new district of Marif.

The master plan is to get investment downtown again, a long process that's begun with cleaning up the streets and giving the grand old buildings a badly-needed coat of paint. The most important change is that of the mindset, enthusing both locals and visitors about real Casablanca again. And, it's happening. Precious Art Deco treasures are being restored, albeit on a micro scale.

One of the most impressive renovations is the boutique Hotel de la Doge. Tucked away in a narrow cul-de-sac opposite the imposing Sacré Coeur Cathedral, the hotel is a hymn to Art Deco style. The doors are festooned with curled wrought-iron, the furniture and fittings sculpted from sweeping lines. Named after famous celebrities of the time, the sixteen rooms and suites have been painstakingly adorned with period objects – all of them sourced in the city's antique shops and flea markets. The result is a dream-like moment from Titanic, stepping into a pristine 1930s Casablanca.

11722395R00115

Made in the USA
San Bernardino, CA
27 May 2014